MAHATMA GANDHI'S THOUGHT:

Philosophy of Truth and Nonviolence

Ramesh N. Patel

~ * ~

Lok Sangrah Prakashan

Loka-sangraham evapi sampashyan kartum arhasi

Mahatma Gandhi's Thought:
Philosophy of Truth and Nonviolence

by Ramesh N. Patel

Lok Sangrah Prakashan

ISBN # 9798686070899

Contact: rameshphilosophy@gmail.com
Info: www.amazon.com/author/rameshpatel

Printed in the U.S.A.

Acknowledgement:
Permission is gratefully acknowledged from Jitendra Desai of Navajivan Trust, Amdavad, to translate and publish excerpts from Kishorlal G. Mashruwala's *Gandhi-Vichar-Dohan*, per letter of January 28, 1991.

To:

Three great women
Who made the Mahatma

Putliba, Mahatma's mother,
Rambha, Mahatma's childhood
confidant and
Kasturba, Mahatma's wife.

They taught him
Austerity,
God's name and
Non-violence.

And the rest is history.

Books by Professor Ramesh N. Patel:

One Being: Spiritual Path of Adi Shankara, Lok Sangrah Prakashan, 2020. $9.95. 129 pages.

Self and World: Major Aspects of Indian Philosophy, Lok Sangrah Prakashan, 2020. $9.95. 125 pages.

Spiritual Stories: Inspiring Messages of Wisdom, Lok Sangrah Prakashan, 2020. 119 pages.

Mahatma Gandhi's Thought: Philosophy of Truth and Nonviolence, Lok Sangrah Prakashan, 2020. 121 pages.

Hindu Philosophy of Life: Meaning of Life in Hinduism, Lok Sangrah Prakashan, 2020. 164 pages.

Seeing One in Many: A Dialog in Hindu Spirituality for Today, Lok Sangrah Prakashan, 2020. 392 pages.

Hinduism for Today, Abiding Publications, 2012. 436 pages. Out of print.

Philosophy of the Gita, Peter Lang, New York, 1991. 311 pages.

Contact: rameshphilosophy@gmail.com
Info: www.amazon.com/author/rameshpatel

MAHATMA GANDHI'S THOUGHT:
Philosophy of Truth and Nonviolence

Ramesh N. Patel

CONTENTS

CHAPTER ONE

MAKING OF THE MAHATMA

The great poet and Nobel Laureate Rabindra Nath Tagore is said to be the first to use the appellation "Mahatma," which means "great soul" for Mohandas Karamchand Gandhi in 1915. Ever since, "Mahatma Gandhi" is the way the father of the nation of India or Bharat has been known. When the title "Mahatma" is not used, he is respectfully called "Gandhiji." This book will use these two terms, in the main, to refer to the Mahatma: Mahatma Gandhi, Gandhiji.

Kunverji-bhai and Kalyanji-bhai Mehta, my mother's uncles, together with Prabhu-bhai Mehta, who was known as Mangal-bhai, my mother's father, worked closely with Gandhiji and participated in Gandhiji's civil disobedience movement to pursue India's independence from the British rule. If they would catch me ever saying just "Gandhi", they would reprimand me severely, and correctly, for it is quite disrespectful to call the Mahatma just "Gandhi."

Once, Mohamed Ali Jinna, the Muslim leader who was a political opponent of Gandhiji, addressed him as "Mr. Gandhi." The audience, a large crowd, protested Gandhiji being addressed so disrespectfully but Gandhiji, with his characteristic humility, pacified the crowd and said that "Mr. Gandhi" was a respectable way to address him.

` Mahatma Gandhi himself never liked or approved the appellation "Mahatma," but resigned to it as popular will. Not knowing this cultural background, Westerners and even some Westernized Indians have made a routine of calling him just

"Gandhi." Even Richard Attenborough's remarkable movie is titled "Gandhi." Ignorance of the law is no excuse, but what about ignorance of cultural protocol? Whatever. Knowing the norm or protocol myself, I see no reason to be offensive and obnoxious, trying to get away with "Gandhi." So, it will be Mahatma Gandhi or Gandhiji here.

Oh, there is more! Things are never simple! Gandhiji was very lovingly called "Bapu," which means "father." That is how he became "father of the nation." It was Netaji Subhash Chandra Bose who called him "Rashtra-pita" first, in 1944. "Rashtra-pita" means father of the nation. People also refer to Gandhiji as "Gandhi-bapu." And that is pretty respectable, too. "Gandhi Mahatma" is yet another venerable way of referring to him. So, we can respectfully call Gandhiji, all these: Gandhiji, Mahatma Gandhi, Bapu, Gandhi-bapu.

But, what if one calls him "Gandhi" without meaning any disrespect? Is it bad in itself, regardless of cultural protocol? Of course not. In English, calling one by just the last name is formal and is not necessarily disrespectful. But saying it with the prefix "Mister" makes it formally respectable. However, just "Gandhi" is disrespectful in India for Gandhiji, because of his special situation as father of the nation and his universally honored greatness.

The word "gandhi" means "grocer." Maybe, Gandhiji's ancestors were grocers and adopted that as their last name. How about just his first name, Mohandas? Even there, there are variations! "Mohandas" is the full name, like Robert. His friends and family would hardly call him by that name. They would rather say "Mohan," like Robert would be called Bob. "Mohan" is a name for Shri-Krishna, God-incarnate in Hinduism, meaning "spellbinder," one who casts a spell on you through his beauty, grace and love. "Mohandas" means servant of Mohan, that is of God. Gandhiji's mother, Putli-ba, called him "Moniyo" with playful love.

Notice that I said "Putli-ba" and not the usual "Putli-bai." "Bai" means lady. "Ba" means mother. Kastur-ba, Gandhiji's wife, was called "Ba" by all in India, revering her status as the mother of the nation. Hence, "Ba" is more appropriate than "Bai." While "bai" indicates normal respect, "ba" adds closeness and endearment.

Is this enough fuss about name and how to call the man who was the runner-up for Time magazine's greatest or most consequential person of the twentieth century? We know the contest ended up as the match between Einstein and Gandhiji. Einstein won, of course. But for a non-Westerner to get to that level was phenomenal. Also remember what Einstein said about Mahatma Gandhi when the latter was assassinated in 1948: "Generations to come will scarce believe that such a one as this ever in flesh and blood walked upon this earth."

So, it's not just the cultural protocol or good manners. The need to prefer "Gandhiji," "Mahatma Gandhi" and "Bapu" is really about respecting greatness. It is amusing to see so many still write about Gandhiji as if he was just another politician. Was Jesus just a carpenter? It seems to show vanity more than propriety. But what can one say?

Why was he great? By what standards? Who decides? Well, how much weight should we place on this matter on the elite, sophistry-laden analytical class of pundits? Intellectuals tend to be a contentious bunch, overall. They have not performed well on the pivotal concept in the Mahatma's thought: his concept of truth. A whole lot more about it later.

The first, foremost and incontrovertible reason to regard him as a great person is of course his leading role in gaining independence for India from the British colonial rule. And this liberation of the second most populous nation in the world was achieved primarily through Gandhiji's nonviolent civil resistance and not through the hitherto normal military or otherwise violent means.

True, there are many detractors of Gandhiji here too, who try to minimize or underplay his role in both the leadership he exerted and how nonviolent was the movement he led. But if you ask people themselves rather than ivory tower captives who claim to write so-called history, these denizens of academia will seem trying to pull wool over people's eyes, seeking in vain to minimize Gandhiji's leadership role in India's struggle for independence or on the nonviolent nature of the struggle. They better show one good clear example of a civil nonviolent resistance any time in history of the world where this happened before, or even after, for that matter.

But there is more to his greatness than just even this big piece of history. Gandhiji ruled over the hearts of millions and millions of people that is unimaginable in this cynical day and age. Politicians may get a lot of popularity, but they hardly get spontaneous love from people. Gandhiji commanded historically unprecedented love from people. The deep bond of love between him and the people was something that the British government through its machinations always was the most afraid of.

The story of the Mahatma's greatness has to be understood through how he got to the hearts of the people. Intellectuals' clever but rather superficial observations of his ideas is not a great clue to understanding the hearts of millions upon millions of people who just loved their Bapu dearly. They included lots of people who opposed him politically and still loved him so much. You do not earn this type of respect, love and, yes, greatness, by mere intelligence and clever thinking that intellectuals should be good at.

I was nine years old when the news was flashed that Gandhiji was assassinated. I remember young and old, everyone around, crying, shedding tears spontaneously. I saw life-long conservative Hindus, who opposed Gandhiji, crying like babies on hearing about his passing. I saw this first hand. National mourning was declared lasting for a week. We went to school daily for about ten days, only to form lines for walking all over the town, singing devotional songs incorporating themes from different religions of the world, for Gandhiji respected and honored all the major world religions. You could hear nothing but such devotional songs on the radio day or night for a week.

Some intellectuals good at shuffling abstract notions but with little desire to fathom human depth are apt to remark that those children were just forced to assemble and proceed in lines to walk the streets of India's towns. Far from it. I was in fifth grade. But I could see most genuine sorrow on the faces of all adults around the school: teachers, staff and visiting parents. All participated voluntarily and cried spontaneously. It is doubtful if intellectuals have a good understanding of the human language of tears.

They sometimes act like dried-up robots. Gandhiji called them *buddhi-jivi*, parasites living on intellect. If you are one, take heart, I am one of you! I have been there and done that. A professor of philosophy for more than thirty years! True, I have been an intellectual, sort of, but also rather a dissident and iconoclastic one. I have hardly been the establishment type of intellectual. Teaching at a maverick anti-establishment place like Antioch College averted that fate for me. Luckily. I have known intellectuals intimately, so many of them are friends. Good human beings but, when they write for the so-called professional journals, a few of them tend to leave their humanity behind aspiring to be rather peer-reviewed parrots.

The openly crying crowd of more than two million joined the funeral procession for the Mahatma. The noted poet-saint Kabir said this in his immortal poetry several hundred years ago: when you were born, you cried and the world rejoiced; live such life that when you die, you rejoice and people cry." By this standard of greatness, Gandhiji is readily one of the greatest persons in recorded history, for, a pretty large number of people spontaneously cried hearing about his death. Who knows if something like it has happened before him. Nobody knows but there is no way we can rule out the possibility it may happen again in future.

Let's look at a Hindu traditional mark of greatness. For, Gandhiji was raised as a Hindu and claimed to be a Hindu all his life. Not a few thinkers regard him as the greatest Hindu in history. Hindu tradition holds that, if you leave the world with God's name on your lips, you go to God. And such a person is to be respected as a great person. They say that unless you have been good, that is, doing God's good work all your life, you won't have God's name on your lips or in your mind at the time of your death. You would rather be thinking of the major earthly goals that you could not fulfill.

Mahatma was shot three bullets in the chest at point blank range. He is said to have uttered "He Rama" twice as he collapsed and died. That means "O God!" When he was a little child, he was afraid of dark. He revealed this fear to his confidant, Rambha by name, who was the nanny in the house. She asked him to keep saying "Rama" while entering dark, to avoid fear. Little Mohan did that and his fear was gone. He grew up to be one of the most fearless in history. But his habit of saying Rama constantly did not last long. It faded. Yet, when he remembered it again, he constantly practiced saying Rama all the time while awake. One can say it kept him aware of God all through his waking hours. So it is that God's name came to his lips at his last moment on the earth. That's the Hindu traditional mark of greatness.

Okay, okay, but how can you say all these things about Mahatma Gandhi so positively and definitively? What is your line of special access to him, if any? There are Gandhian scholars and Gandhian thinkers who have devoted their life to studying and pondering Gandhiji's thought. Are they not good enough for everybody? Why do we need you talking about Gandhiji on top of these experts' prodigious output?

Fair enough questions. Thinking about the Gandhian scholars and thinkers and their voluminous output, certainly makes me humble, very humble. Indeed, you can say I have the audacity to say things about Gandhiji positively and definitively. Let me lay out some background to, hopefully, lessen the audacity somewhat.

Gandhiji himself was a prolific writer. How prolific? Very prolific. And that is quite an understatement. The "Collected Works of Mahatma Gandhi," published with truly laborious and industrious work by a team of scholars for many years, took 98 large volumes! That's "prolific" in any dictionary. Besides, his writing is simple, unassuming and crystal clear. It is amusing that some intellectuals would profess to "interpret" it to anybody. But, what can you do or say? After all, there are abstruse theological commentaries written on the Bible, which too is such a simple and beautifully clear document.

The point is that Gandhiji does not really need any "interpreter" to get himself understood where he stands on any issue. And he touched on a host of issues pertaining to life. Hence, in seemingly adding to these intellectual interpretations I would definitely appear to be thrashing the grain which has already been thrashed enough.

To this my plea is that Gandhiji has not succeeded in clearly communicating his own most important idea, that of truth, generally but particularly to the intelligentsia. Subsequently, the intellectual class devolved on the second most concept that he emphasized, that of nonviolence. A lot more about this later, which is one of the major reasons for my writing this book.

There are other audacity-reducing reasons, though, and I will not claim any credit for them. They rather are happenstance blessings which just fell on me. I will note three of them: family, language and locality.

I have already referred to the family connections to Gandhiji I had. The mother's side of my family, particularly my mother's father and two uncles, were close associates of Gandhiji and participated in Gandhiji's civil disobedience movement against the British rule of India. As a result, their property was confiscated by the British who threw them in jail. My mother, Sumatiben, was thrown out on the streets at the age of thirteen.

But they survived. On release from the jail, my maternal grand-father, known as Nana by all, asked Gandhiji what he and his two co-worker friends should do. Bapu told them to serve the cows. What a beautiful concept they picked up from him and followed it up! The three partners started with three animals and by their entrepreneurial efforts grew the dairy business to 3,000 animals. They named their Gandhiji-inspired dairy farm "Adarsh Dugdhalaya," meaning ideal dairy farm.

Adarsh dairy gained tremendous reputation in the wider Mumbai area. More importantly, not a single cow was ever sent to the slaughter house. Every cow died a natural death, grazing grass on the dairy's farmland. Contrast this with the usual practice of similar businesses to send any and every cow to be slaughtered the moment she stops yielding milk. I played around a lot on the Adarsh dairy farm as a child.

Gandhiji and his family used to visit Adarsh. I was born in Mumbai. I am told I was a cry baby! I was in a hammock style cradle. Gandhiji's son Ramdas pulled the string on my cradle and swung me several times. My mom called him Ramdas-kaka, meaning Uncle Ramdas. I met him several times as I grew up. If I remember it right, Gandhiji himself cradled me once too.

Anyway, as an infant, I have played in the lap of Kastur-ba Gandhi, mother of the nation and Gandhiji's wife, several times! She was one of the earliest to call me by my first name, Ramesh. How sweet that would have been! But I did not know what was happening to me. Little would Kastur-ba realize that she was playing with an infant who would grow up to teach a course on her husband's thinking, in the U.S.A.!

Adarsh tried to emulate many features of a typical Gandhian ashram or commune. We used to have morning and evening prayers regularly, with the families living nearby gathering to pray. Later, morning prayers were canceled because of people's crowded schedule. Many Gandhian workers used to visit from time to time. Many children traditionally grow up in India at their maternal uncle's place. I did not entirely, though I can say I nearly did, for I spent almost all school vacations at Nana's Adarsh. Kunverji-bhai, the elder uncle of my mother, lived nearby, a few blocks away. Kalyanji-bhai, the other uncle, who remained very active in social and political work, founded his own Gandhian commune, which was inaugurated by Gandhiji himself and was named Kasturba Sevashram, after Kastur-ba.

Kastur-ba's brother, Madhavdas, lost fortune in stock market and had no family to fall back upon. He was depressed for a while, even suicidal. Gandhiji and Kastur-ba both were in jail and were worried about him, particularly because he was difficult to take care of and had no place to go.

Kunverji-bhai asked Gandhiji if he could take care of Madhavdas. Gandhiji warned him how difficult he would be but Kunverji-bhai promised Gandhiji that he would take diligent care of him. He brought Madhavdas to his own home in Mumbai in 1945. Madhavdas was called "Mama," by everybody: "Mama" means mother's brother. Very apt calling for the brother of the mother of the nation.

I got to see Madhavdas-mama all the time I frequented Kunverji-bhai's home to meet and play with the latter's grand-children, my cousins, who were in my age-group. Once, when I went to see them, they were all in a prayer meeting, which I joined. Madhavdas-mama sang the bhajan, devotional song, "*Raghu-bar tum ko meri laj*," at the meeting. I vividly remember that still. He spoke very little, but he was very nice with us children. Kunverji-bhai's family took care of him for life, because they had promised Gandhiji that they would do so. Mama lived with Kunverji-bhai's family for seventeen years.

I say "Kunverji-bhai" with trepidation. Everybody knew him as "Bapuji." Similarly, "Kalyanji-bhai" is an audacious way to refer to my mother's uncle, whom everyone knew as "Kaka," which means Uncle. Both were like pillars of our extended family. We all sought their guidance in all important matters. Political luminaries used to visit them all the time. Both were close to Gandhiji and Sardar Patel. Kaka always addressed me as Pandit, referencing my prowess in Sanskrit. Both, when available in their very busy activist life, shared their memories of Gandhiji with us children.

As I said, family, language and locality were three of the reasons I have the audacity to talk positively and definitively about the Mahatma. The latter spoke Gujarati, a language spoken in the state of Gujarat in Western India. Gandhiji was born in Gujarat and Gujarati was his native language. I was born in Mumbai, nearby, and was raised in Gujarat, speaking Gujarati.

When I grew up, during my school years, we had a number of books written by Gandhiji and his co-workers. Almost all of them were written in Gujarati. I read them avidly. I particularly want to mention Gandhiji's autobiography, called *Atma-katha*, in two volumes. *Satyamay Jivan* or Life of Truth, *Ahimsa Vivechan* or Analysis of Nonviolence and *Gandhi Vichar Dohan* or Quintessence of Gandhiji's Thought were other serious works, along with some more, on Gandhiji's thought that I sought to peruse and ponder in my high school years.

This early access to first-hand sources of Gandhism in the native language of the Mahatma and his co-workers had helped me immensely in understanding Gandhism deeply enough to avoid and overcome distortions of translation in English. Very often, English translations of primary Gujarati sources of Gandhism leave out details and nuances which make a material difference in comprehension.

Of course, I was exposed to a great deal of Gandhi literature during my school and college years. As students, we constantly talked about Gandhiji and his thought, throughout the school and college years. Much of this was in Gujarati, although bulk of it started to occur in English as we progressed at college.

So it is that both locality and language played a large role in my access to, and influence from, Gandhiji's writings. Because Gandhiji was from Gujarat, the latter claimed him as its own with great vigor. Interestingly, Gandhiji was claimed by all the regions of India as their own: such was his influence and popularity. Just about everyone loved him dearly.

Another important aspect of locality is the regional culture and its customary practices as well as idiosyncrasies. Being raised in almost the same cultural environment as Gandhiji provided me a sort of edge. One is able to understand certain behavior more easily and in certain clearer light.

One example may drive this point. home. As I referred to it in a somewhat different context, a child often was almost raised at its maternal uncle's place. The immense significance of this is lost on those who do not know this source of impact on a person's development. In the case of Gandhiji's children, this had a tremendous particular influence that was largely missed by many Gandhian scholars.

Since Gandhiji left India for England and later for South Africa, his children grew up under the influence of their maternal uncles even more strongly than otherwise. They were subjected to strong impact from their two uncles who impressed upon them the idea that their father was going to make a lot of money and they would be rolling in luxuries for their life without having to do much to earn a living themselves.

When the children finally faced Gandhiji's austere lifestyle in South Africa, they were shell-shocked and revolted. They were extremely difficult to handle. They gave Gandhiji a very hard time staying his course of minimal, austere and simple living that he volunteered to practice, foregoing the usual goal of amassing riches. His chosen lifestyle involved working on a farm and doing physical menial labor. Dignity of labor was anathema to the way children were taught by their uncles.

Children expecting a very easy life just could not stomach austerity, let alone understand its deep spirituality. Their mother tried to explain, supporting their father. But the dice was already thrown by the uncles and was hard to retract. Family was thrown into a crisis.

It is a pity that so many intellectuals and even otherwise sympathetic thinkers have tended to blame Gandhiji entirely for being too stern with children and neglecting their good and developmental needs. Their painting of Gandhiji as self-absorbed and negligent of parental care is almost a hoax. If you have to deal with children brought up elsewhere to become spoiled brats, you would not know how to manage them, especially if your philosophy of life is way ahead in moral and spiritual sensibility.

Yes, one can argue about this. But it is a clear case of conflict of values. Does parental duty mean and include having to reverse your own lifestyle totally to satisfy a child's stubborn demands of affluence? To what extent you should go trying to meet your children's lifestyle preferences? Do your values and preferences not count at all? How many people are willing to materially alter their life goals and ways so that their children can live a luxurious life? How many should? If you do, you would be living for your children during your youthful and productive years. Do you not have a right to your own life?

It is easy to cast stones at other people's houses from your own glass houses. Lots of people end up with divorces in these situations. Maybe Gandhiji could have been more tactful and less stern. He was just learning nonviolence at that point. To imply that he should live for his children rather than for himself when there is a clear conflict between the two is just playing upon readers' parental emotions. Intellectuals' rather shameless admonition of Gandhiji here is not as obviously meritorious as they claim it to be. This understanding of Gandhiji's plight is a good example about an edge for knowing a bit about shared local cultural traits.

Now that I have spoken about family, language and locality that brought me closer to understanding the Mahatma, so that I can "audaciously" speak about Gandhiji positively and definitively, I should restate that I do not deserve any credit for them. I happened to be there and they fell on me, kind of. Yes, I absorbed these blessings.

As far as the making of the Mahatma is concerned, a lot has been written. But the most important of this literature is Gandhiji's autobiography, what he subtitled "My Experiments in Truth." It has been tremendously influential in itself. It has impacted millions of people's lives beneficially. The details narrated in it about how Gandhiji developed in his search for truth are clearly laid out in the work.

So, I will be forgiven for not repeating them here. Suffice it to say, influence from the Hindu stories of Lord Rama, King Harischandra, the child Prahlada and such impacted the child Mohandas greatly and causally, propelling him toward greatness. In his adolescent and adult life, there were other notable influences like his study of the Hindu scripture *Bhagavad-gita* and the scriptures of world religions. Gandhiji particularly found the Biblical Sermon on the Mount deeply moving and inspirational. Among people who influenced him, Raichandbhai, John Ruskin and Leo Tolstoy must be mentioned.

I must state and emphasize the role of three great women in the making of the Mahatma: Putli-ba who was Gandhiji's mother, Rambha who was his childhood confidant and Kastur-ba who was his life partner. Putli-ba was an austere woman. She used to observe vows in the customary Hindu tradition. An example is often mentioned, sourced from his autobiography.

Putli-ba had a vow that she would not eat until she had a glimpse, called *darshan* in Gujarati, of the Sun. Her children, including Gandhiji whom she called Moniyo, would wait for the Sun to come out of clouds during monsoon and would call her out when it was clearly visible. Mother would rush out from her daily chores to see the Sun and the Sun would go back into the clouds before she could see it. She would just say, maybe God did not want her to eat for the day. She would quietly go back to her work and be absorbed in it. The sensitive Mohandas picked up the value of living austerely with a happy mood and face from his mother.

I have already narrated the contribution of Rambha to Gandhiji's development in the context of his speaking God's name at the time of his death. Gandhiji used to say that he should be called Mahatma only if he would be able to take bullets on his chest and still would have God's name on his lips. Well, Rambha's teaching him of *Rama-nama* or God's name certainly did this for him at the end of his life.

Last, but not the least, was his third female guru, his wife, Kastur-ba. The latter was very headstrong, had her own mind and would not obey anyone who asked her to do otherwise. This caused a storm in the early married life of the Gandhi couple. Later, in South Africa, where the couple got to know each other much better, Kastur-ba would still refuse to change her mind just to accommodate her husband's dominant will. Dispute would erupt, leading to great tension. Gandhiji would exert his male pressure of the husband, but Kastur-ba would not budge. She continued displaying nonviolent resistance and would ultimately emerge successful and effective.

After a while, experiencing and observing many instances of his wife succeeding in her nonviolent resistance, it dawned on Gandhiji that nonviolence can be a truly effective method in conflict situations. He became convinced of the efficacy of nonviolence as a conflict-resolving tool. He then thought of extending it to the social and political sphere. If it was effective at the domestic level, he asked himself, why could it not be so outside the home? And that was the birth of his globally celebrated method of truth-insistence or *satyagraha*. He learnt the value and efficacy of nonviolence at the socio-political level from Kastur-ba.

Seems clear that the impact of these three female gurus of Gandhiji played a significant role in the making of the Mahatma. Gandhiji did not have a formal guru or personal spiritual guide in the traditional way that it works in Hinduism. But the role played by the three relatively unsung great women in his life was no less inspirational and impactful in his transformation toward greatness than the customary role of a guru in a Hindu's life.

Several events and episodes revealed by Gandhiji himself in his autobiography have been made meanspirited and even diabolical use of by some so-called intellectuals or scholars to badmouth Gandhiji. Particularly, relating to his passionate sexual drive. There is a saying in Hindi *meri billi aur mujh ko meow*, meaning "my own cat threatening me with a meow." Shame on these little mind-vultures merrily feeding on things revealed by Gandhiji alone without whom nobody would have even known them.

The scholars sound amateurish, trying to practice long-distance psychologizing from across cultures and generations, applying their culture's values blindly to Gandhiji's childhood and development. Licentious child-abuse? There is no need to dignify these pretentious and offensive shenanigans with a serious reference, let alone study!

Now to relate some of my personal experiences that led me to study Gandhiji's thought more closely. My mother was a Gandhian reformist Hindu and my father was a self-made conservative Hindu. Both my father and Gandhiji were lawyers by profession. Growing up in such a family made me to compare and contrast two sides of the Hindu view and way of life. I have been torn often enough, but I believe it also exposed me to what is good, positive and constructive on both sides, so that I would not be easily pulled into one just by its rhetoric.

It was a night in April, 1983 when a faculty colleague of mine at Antioch College woke me up little past midnight. He screamed at me as he called me on telephone, "Ramesh, your Gandhi killed my ET.!" I reminded him of Gandhiji's nonviolence to no avail! Obviously, he was complaining about the movie Gandhi bagging many Oscar awards, depriving another great wholesome movie called ET.

My major complaint about the movie Gandhi was that Gandhiji's spirituality was very scantily depicted in the film. I learnt, though, that Attenborough wanted to show it adequately, but he was dissuaded by the Government of India which wanted him to project a secular image of the Father of the Nation. Politicians! Another bunch with its shenanigans.

Anyway, it was soon after the movie was released and became very popular that my senior colleague, Al Denman, the best teacher I have ever seen, asked me if I could teach a course on Gandhiji's thought. There already was a seminar in Antioch's philosophy curriculum called "Violence and Nonviolence." Al said I could offer a Gandhi course right away without faculty approval and as a title in the pre-existing seminar. I was hesitant and circumspect, wondering if there was sufficient demand for a course on Gandhiji's thought.

Undaunted, Al arranged for a community meeting under a weekly program he was managing, called Friday Forum. He invited me to speak at the meeting. A flood of people showed up.

I spoke to the large group which was greatly enthusiastic about Gandhiji's ideas.

I talked to them about how Kunverji-bhai, my maternal grand-uncle regarded Gandhiji as an incarnation of God and how Gandhiji tried hard but in vain to dissuade him in that belief and from spreading such belief. At a community meeting, Gandhiji reprimanded him for spreading the belief that Gandhiji was God. He even said that Kunverji committed an unforgivable offense in calling Gandhiji God.

To this, Kunverji-bhai pleaded that he was telling people just what he truly believed. Gandhiji would not have any of it and asked Kunverji-bhai to retract in public and promise him that he won't call Gandhiji as God to anybody. In my talk, I too emphasized how Gandhiji was strongly opposed to him being called God, because, for one, he thought people would not follow his ideas in real life, thinking that he as God could do it but ordinary mortals cannot practice such high-demanding ideas. Besides, he emphatically rejected the idea that he was God in any sense of the term.

As I finished the talk and the following question-and-answer session, a middle-aged Black woman walked up to me, shook my hand and thanked me for speaking about Gandhiji. But she sternly told me point blank: "Good try, professor, but I am not persuaded. He was God."

I was stunned. But I decided to teach Gandhi course, seeing that there was a great demand for learning the Mahatma's ideas and nonviolent methods of practicing them. Later, with ready faculty approval, I made it a regular philosophy offering with the title "Gandhi: Truth and Nonviolence." I taught the course for eighteen straight years. It was not just a very highly popular course at Antioch, it was one of my most memorable courses I ever taught. The kind of deeply sensitive and sincere type of students it drew was astounding. Some students went to India and lived at Gandhian ashrams or communes. They practiced many of Gandhian ideas in their own creative ways. Their experience in India and earnest attempt to live Gandhian ideas in the U.S.A. has left a deep impression on me. I have even learned from talking to them over years.

Of course, we saw the movie Gandhi every time I taught the course. Typically, we would view it at the beginning of the course after I gave the students brief introduction to Gandhiji's life and work. But as we studied the Mahatma for several months, they often wanted to see the film again. When we viewed the film again, they told me they got so much more out of it because of the learning they had acquired about him.

I taught a variety of books on Gandhiji through those eighteen years of teaching the Gandhi course. This too made me to learn a whole lot more each time I taught the course. Once we spotted Arun Gandhi, a grand-son of Gandhiji, visiting nearby. We invited him to our meeting. It was an exciting event. Overall, teaching Gandhi course for eighteen years has been a treasure of experience for me. It enhanced my knowledge of Gandhiji's thinking and also deepened my understanding of it. Still, I must say I cannot get over feeling some audacity in talking positively and definitively about Gandhiji in this book. But many people have for many years asked me to write about Gandhiji's thought. So, here it is, whatever its worth. Many Gandhian thinkers have spent a lifetime studying Gandhian thought and I respect their contribution greatly.

After retiring from teaching at Antioch College, I have been teaching voluntary classes in the Bhagavad-gita, Upanishads, Hinduism and Spirituality Studies, under auspices of the Hindu Temple of Dayton. I have offered four week-end workshops over the last decade or so, to the Dayton area community. The first of these workshops was on Mahatma Gandhi's thought, hosted graciously by Krishnakantbhai and Yoginiben Patel. Parts of this book derive from that workshop's material.

The most intriguing part of Mahatma Gandhi's thought for me for long has been his innovative dual concept of truth. It is not just a remarkably original idea. It is ethically the most challenging and demanding concept in the history of humanity, East and West. The very thought of practicing it, actually living it in real life, for just a week or so is apt to numb the mind. Think of Gandhiji in that light, who actually lived it for decades to the end of his life, ever since he devised it, practicing it day in and day out, without a single day of relaxation or vacation. That's called greatness: Is there anything that shines more brightly in the known history of humanity?

Going back to Kunverji-bhai and his belief that Gandhiji was God, it should be stated that it was not an uncommon belief. Millions have believed it, and strongly, for that matter. Kunverji-bhai was not particularly religious, so let us go into his belief a little more deeply.

Kunverji-bhai visited Kastur-ba when she was in jail at Aga Khan Palace in Pune. She regarded him as her son and told him to reserve a corner in his house where she would like to spend the rest of her life. He confided in her about his belief that Gandhiji was God. Kastur-ba told him that she too believed that Gandhiji was God. She said she went from nobody to being the mother of the nation and that was a miracle that happened only because of Gandhiji.

Kunverji-bhai did not believe Gandhiji being God in the sense that the Mahatma had some God-like powers. He rather thought that Gandhiji had perfected his vow of nonviolence that could not be done by an ordinary mortal and hence only God could have done it. A real-life event that he witnessed will buttress this.

When Kunverji-bhai was leading Gandhiji's nonviolent resistance movement in the now-historic place called Bardoli, Gandhiji used to visit him from time to time to guide strategy and planning. Once, when Gandhiji was visiting, Kunverji-bhai spotted a hefty and fearsome Pathan roaming around the commune, wielding a large knife. Several members of the commune suspected that he may have been sent by the British government to kill Gandhiji.

One day, they confronted the Pathan and asked him why he was loitering around the commune. He said with disdain that he could walk any public place and nobody could stop him. They pointed out that the place he was treading was a private property of the commune. He then said he was looking for Gandhi Mahatma but found that the latter was always busy with someone. He said he wanted to see Gandhiji in a personal meeting.

When Gandhiji was told about this, he wanted to see him in private as the Pathan wished. Everyone, particularly Kunverji-bhai, was wary, fearing for Gandhiji's life. But as Gandhiji insisted, they let the Pathan approach Gandhiji in a private meeting. They hid themselves outside the room where the meeting occurred. What they saw happen stunned them for life.

The Pathan approached Gandhiji and asked him about his vow of nonviolence, saying it is not possible that anybody can successfully and effectively stay nonviolent in his heart, especially under provocation. Gandhiji said in response that indeed it was difficult but that his heart is pure and at peace with everybody in the world with no trace of hatred or ill will toward anyone. The Pathan pointed to his big knife and said he wanted to cut off Gandhiji's nose with it.

Gandhiji bowed his head down and said in a tone that had no fear and was the voice of his soul, "O brother, if it pleases you, you can even cut off my head. Here it is in front of you." Kunverji-bhai and his associates were so impacted that they thought only the Buddha, Mahavira or Jesus would be able to speak those words with utter sincerity ringing in them.

The Pathan melted right at the moment, threw away his knife and started to cry. He apologized to Gandhiji for misjudging him and underestimating the strength of his vow of nonviolence. The commune members rushed in and knew they had witnessed a miracle. Kunverji-bhai said that no one who witnessed this event would ever forget it. He also said this perfection in the vow of nonviolence was the reason why he believed that Gandhiji was God. And that only someone with pure love for everybody in his heart could do this and it would take God to be able to do it.

The sage Patanjali wrote the famous classic in yoga called *Yoga-sutra*. There is one *sutra* or aphorism in that classic work which goes like this in Sanskrit: *Ahimsa-pratishthayam tat sannidhau vaira-tyagah*. It means: Enmity ends in the vicinity of one who is established in nonviolence. Commenting on it, Gandhiji has said that this is not just a bookish statement, for when a person is truly established in nonviolence and has no trace of hatred or violence left in his mind and heart, it won't be surprising if even born enemies like cat and mouse would give up their enmity when they are close to him or her.

The Mahatma could have easily become the President or Prime Minister of India for life, if he wanted to, after India became independent from the British rule. But he chose to remain one of the millions of private citizens. When he died, he left nothing but his glasses, a few loin cloths and a watch to keep time as all his physical bequest for the humanity.

It has been said that Jawaharlal Nehru who was the first Prime Minister of independent India and Vinoba Bhave who led the land gift movement were like Gandhiji's political and spiritual heirs respectively. Worldwide, three leaders of nonviolent resistance movements have been pointed out as following in Gandhiji's foot-steps: Martin Luther King, Jr. in the U.S.A., Nelson Mandela in South Africa and Aung San Suu Kyi of Myanmar.

Among Gandhiji's favorite devotional songs was "Lead Kindly Light" by Cardinal Newman. At his regular prayer meetings several prayers, chants and devotional songs were rendered. Certain parts formed daily routine, like the nineteen verses at the end of the second chapter of the *Bhagavad-gita.* Gandhiji regarded the *Bhagavad-gita* as his spiritual mother who helped him resolve all kinds of difficult situations as soon as he opened it at any page.

The Mahatma used to get requests from several sources for songs to be included in the multi-language and multi-religion repertoire of devotional songs for his prayer meetings. Narayan Moreshwar Khare was entrusted with the charge for this. He was the musician at Gandhiji's Sabarmati Ashram commune and belonged to the illustrious Gwalior Gharana. He asked Gandhiji on how to select prayer songs for the commune from among so many requests.

Gandhiji gave him three rules to apply for inclusion in the repertoire which was published as *Ashram Bhajanavali:* Exclude a candidate song which demeaned any group of people, which demeaned women in particular and which resorted to temptation or threat to induce belief. Gandhiji noticed that many religious songs tended to blame women for provoking sexual thought in them just because of their female body. He laid the blame on men themselves for this. He also noticed that quite a few offered heaven as a big carrot and hell as a big stick to make people to believe in their doctrines. Gandhiji would exclude those too. Of course, discrimination against any group was obvious reason for exclusion.

It is well-known that one song in particular, *Vaishnav Jan*, was one of his most favorite. It lists the qualities, attributes and traits of behavior of a Godly person. We have spent time on why Gandhiji was the Mahatma, a great soul. This song tells us what Gandhiji himself regarded as ideals for a great soul. Here is my translation of the Gujarati poem-song with a small introduction.

Narsinh Mehta, the first Gujarati poet, lived in Junagadh in Western India nearly four centuries ago. He wrote devotional poetry. He was an exceptionally sensitive devotee of Lord Krishna. His life as we know it is filled with legendary accounts of the helping hand he received from Krishna when his devotion left him no time for social customs and the society persecuted him for neglecting the customs. He is fondly called Narsaiyo. Narsaiyo would go anywhere to sing his devotional songs, even in the community of the "untouchables." His poetry exhibits a deep grasp of the conceptual structure of the subtle aspects of the spiritual philosophy of Vedantic Hinduism. At the same time, it is couched in utterly simple language.

Here is a poem-song, which describes the qualities of a truly Godly person. It lays down the ethical attributes of the Godly person and refrains from laying down any structure of theological beliefs he or she must have. This is why it was a favorite of Mahatma Gandhi who regarded it as adequately summarizing his own philosophy of life, which, unlike many, he actually practiced. The original Gujarati is followed by a liberal translation.

Vaishnav jan to tene re kahiye, je pid parai jane re
Par dukkhe upakar kare toye, man abhiman na ane re

A godly person is sensitive to others' suffering, rewards a harm-doer with help and yet does not let pride enter the mind.

Sakal lok man sahune vande, ninda na kare keni re
Vach kachh man nishchal rakhe, dhan dhan janani teni re

This one reveres all in the whole world, does not call anyone names, is consistent in words, deeds, and thoughts; such a person's mother deserves utter reverence.

Sama drushti ne trushna tyagi, para-stri jene mata re

Jihva thaki asatya na bole, para-dhan nava jhale hath re

Such a one regards all as equals, is devoid of craving, respects every woman as one's own mother, does not let untruth slip out of mouth, and never lays hands on another's wealth.

Moha maya vyape nahi jene, drudh vairagya jena man man re
Ram nam shun tali re lagi, sakal tirath tena tan man re

Such a person is one whom confusion and distraction do not overwhelm, one whose mind is firmly unattached, one who is engrossed in chanting God's name; in this person's body dwell the holiness of everything holy.

Vana-lobhi ne kapata rahita chhe, kama krodh nivaryan re,
Bhane Narasaiyo enu darshan kartan, kul ekoter taryan re

That one is without greed or deception, has overcome lust and anger. Narasaiyo says just the sight of this person is enough to liberate your seventy-one generations.

CHAPTER TWO

TRUTH ABOUT GANDHIJI'S TRUTH

Mahatma Gandhi insisted that truth was the foundational concept of his thought. Gandhian scholars have attempted without success to identify and decipher this concept with a satisfactory degree of clarity and precision. Consequently, they have devolved on the analysis of another foundational but more specific concept in Gandhiji's thought, namely, nonviolence. Gandhiji worked with a two-pronged concept of truth from which he logically derived the concept of nonviolence. Regardless of whether the dual concept of truth has the expected clarity and precision, it can be articulated to the point of shedding considerable elucidatory light on the foundations of Gandhiji's thought.

The ethical structure that emerges from the foundations is distinct from the familiar structures of utilitarian and deontological ethics. Utilitarian ethics offers greatest happiness of the greatest number as the touchstone of the ethical validity of an action. According to it, something is good or an action is right if it promotes or produces the greatest good of the greatest number. For example, a legislation that creates jobs for the people.

Deontological ethics, on the other hand, advocates performance of duty rather than production of happiness as the standard to judge whether an action is ethical. According to it, an action is right if it is performed as a duty, regardless of what, if anything, it produces. For instance, speaking the truth in all circumstances, regardless of where the chips may fall, done as one's duty. Gandhiji's idea of truth, it is remarkable to notice, does not follow either of these two leading theories of ethics.

Gandhiji's moral thought, at its foundational level, rather has elements of intuitionism, situationism, relativism, objectivism and, above all, activism. To explain. It relies on human intuition for its occurrence and validity. It depends a good deal on situation. Every situation has its own unique aspects. So, Gandhiji's perception of moral truth may change depending on the situation where an action is being evaluated for moral truth. Gandhiji's judgment of ethical validity may also not be absolute and fixed all the time. It may be relative.

The Mahatma would not regard it as merely subjective, for moral truth in his view does not depend on the performer's thought about the action. Moral truth is objective, not subjective. No action is ethically valid simply because someone thinks so; it has to be right in itself. Mahatmaji tends to regard it as objective, subject to an individual succeeding or failing to grasp it. Finally, for Gandhiji ethical validity consists basically in action which emanates from an activist stance.

But more importantly, Gandhiji's foundational concepts of truth and nonviolence, when understood in his own terms without being reduced to any notions alien to his thinking, imply an ethic that is formidable in its challenge to even the most enterprising human individuals. Indeed, it may be difficult to conceive a more challenging ethic. We will see why this is so.

Interestingly, Gandhiji's own writings do not quite bring out all this in clear terms. One can read his prolific output on the subject but is unlikely to succeed in achieving a clear concept of what the Mahatma is up to in his thinking, on the all-important notion of truth, in particular. This may sound strange and surprising, especially in light of the fact that Gandhiji tended to express himself with great clarity and simplicity.

Let us read from Gandhiji himself on whose writing he considers to be truly reliable and accurately representative of his own foundational thought. After that we will read that person's statement on how it is that this is not found explicitly in Gandhiji's own writings and why his writing represents Gandhiji's thinking more clearly than the Mahatma's writings themselves.

Gandhiji wrote from the town of Borsad on May 20, 1935, translated from Gujarati:

"Approval.

I have read this quintessence of my thought. Brother Kishorlal's familiarity with my thought is extraordinary. Just like his familiarity is his power of comprehension. Hence, I had to make changes only at very few places. Because we both think the same on many subjects, I have had no difficulty in giving my approval to every chapter, even as the language is entirely Kishorlal's. Brother Kishorlal has been able to condense many subjects in brief, which distinguishes his quintessence of my thought."

This is Gandhiji's entire foreword to Kishorlal G. Mashruwala's book called *Gandhi-Vichar-Dohan* or "Quintessence of Gandhi's Thought" written in Gujarati and never translated in English. Mark that it is titled "Approval" by Gandhiji. Kishorlal G. Mashruwala was an intellectually inclined close associate of the Mahatma and lived with the Mahatma in the latter's commune.

He was entrusted to teach Gandhian thought to the entrants into a Gandhian school called Gandhi Vidyalaya in Vile Parle, Mumbai. These entrants were young adults who wanted to go to the villages to serve rural India according to Gandhian principles. His notes for the crash course came to be so highly regarded in the Gandhian community that many asked them to be published for the public benefit. Kishorlal-bhai then arranged them in a logical order and systematic format but would not want to publish them until Gandhiji himself would go over it and seal it with his approval.

Gandhiji was in jail which delayed the reading of the work by him. When he found time to read it through, he made a few changes and approved the work as so changed as accurately representative of his thought. Needless to say, all the changes made by Gandhiji were accepted and adopted in the version to be published as "Quintessence of Gandhi's Thought." It is divided in fourteen sections. Each section is divided in several sub-sections, with every sub-section divided in numerically arranged statements.

It is a very serious and systematic presentation of Gandhiji's thinking on a host of subjects, foundational and topical. Nothing like it exists in the entire Gandhi literature. It is a pity and shame that an English translation of the work has not been published. I have the kind permission of Gandhiji's publisher, Shri. Jitendra Desai of the Navajivan Trust, to translate and publish the *Quintessence* as it is called by Gandhian workers who regard it as the Bible of Gandhi's thought.

Years ago when I was contemplating writing on Gandhiji's thought, I asked Jitendra-bhai why it is that such an extraordinary work like the *Quintessence,* which was called extraordinarily accurate and representative by Gandhiji himself, has not been translated in English. He replied, saying, that the work is so dry, abstruse, tediously systematic and deeply philosophical that nobody has ventured to translate it and many have shied away from the task as too daunting. Acknowledging with gratefulness, Navajivan's permission to translate and publish the *Quintessence*, I regret that there is not enough space to publish the translation in its entirety here. Yet, there are a number of select passages of great importance in the *Quintessence* that appear in this work, for the first time ever in the history of the exposition of the Gandhian thought.

Now let us consider Kishorlal-bhai's own words about Gandhiji's thought. The following is translation from Gujarati preface to the second edition of the book.

"There is hardly any distillation of Gandhiji's writings in this book. It cannot be called a representation of his language or diction. A reader is likely to feel at many places, 'Never saw such anywhere in Gandhiji's own writings.' Hence, really speaking, I have placed in this book in my form and my words the way I have understood the heart and thoughts of Gandhiji." (Page 10)

"There is a lot in this book that is not explicitly in Gandhiji's writings. Is it from the discussion in some of his inner circles? Some may incline to doubt in this way. I would like to say that there is nothing like that. I believe that great people's thoughts cannot be grasped through just the study of their books. You need to associate with them closely. Beyond such association, you need to seek an understanding of their heart. You should make an effort to grasp the foundations at the root of their total mode of thinking. If the foundations can be secured, their whole world of thought becomes obvious like the principles of geometry following from its axioms. This is how I have tried to understand Gandhiji." (Page 11)

Both Gandhiji's and Kishorlal-bhai's words speak for themselves. Just we need to peruse and ponder them with serious attention. What Gandhiji is saying is that Kishorlal-bhai's presentation of his thought is extraordinarily accurate. What Kishorlal-bhai is saying is that his grasp of the Mahatma's thought is not derived from just a study of his writings. It has attained its accuracy by a true grasp of the very foundations of Gandhiji's thought.

From a serious look at both Gandhiji's and Kishorlal-bhai's words, it is evident that the foundation of Gandhiji's thought lies in the concepts of truth and nonviolence, particularly the concept of truth from which Gandhiji claims to have derived the concept of nonviolence. Hence, if we cannot identify such a concept of truth in Gandhiji, we will fail to understand him, no matter how many volumes we read that are written by him.

When studying his own writings is downplayed in this way, studying the commentaries and explanations of scholars and intellectuals is out of question. So, let us try to grasp Gandhiji's concept of truth and the way he derived nonviolence from it. It is downright unimportant whether the derivation is logically rigorous, valid and sound. What is important is how Gandhiji himself understood truth as primarily foundational and nonviolence as derivatively foundational. Intellectuals and their interpretations look so puny in the situation that only a diehard dogmatist would harp on them and that too to his own psychic demise.

Let us draw primarily from Kishorlal G. Mashruwala's *Gandhi-vichar-dohan* (Navajivan, Amdavad, India, 4th edition, 1963), arguably the most authoritative work on Gandhiji's thought. This will show that the all-important concept of truth is not as murky and mystical as alleged by some critics and that one prong of the concept harbors a major innovation in ethical thought and practice.

Further, the conceptual elucidation of Gandhiji's two-pronged truth will clearly imply that attempts at critical evaluation of Gandhiji's ethics have hitherto been seriously handicapped for the lack of insight provided by Mashruwala's work. Among Gandhiji's own associates, Mashruwala was the leading scholar and commentator on Gandhiji's thought.

His *Gandhi-vichar-dohan,* written in Gujarati and not available in English, is held by Gandhians themselves to be the most authoritative work on Gandhiji's thought. Its systematic exposition is characteristic of Mashruwala but uncharacteristic of Gandhiji's own style. Gandhiji went through Mashruwala's work and approved it as authentic exposition of his own thought after making some corrections. Among Gandhians, it has enjoyed greater respect than any other work claiming to elucidate Gandhiji's synoptic thought.

The upshot is that any attempt to understand Gandhiji in terms of concepts not his own is bound to fail by trying to reduce Gandhiji's thought to alien notions. In the following, I attempt to state Gandhiji's ethical foundations in an idiom that avoids any form of reductionism.

Essential and Existential Truth

Truth is the logically necessary beginning of Gandhiji's ethical thought. Gandhiji identifies it with God. He does not identify God with truth, because that can only open the field to doctrinal assertions and counter-assertions of myriad types. Gandhiji's God is not a doctrinal concept. Experiential realization of God, distinct from a credulous conceptualization of God, is for Gandhiji the only but adequate goal of human life. Truth which is God has two aspects one of which is absolute and the other relative. The absolute truth may also be called the essential, transcendental, or metaphysical truth and the relative truth the existential, efficient, or concrete truth.

The essential truth is always and eternally one and the same. It is one without a second. There is nothing else besides it, for it consists of infinite existence. It is all of existence; but it is more. It is infinite consciousness and infinite bliss as well. There is no existence, consciousness, and joy beyond or besides it. It does not have the three, namely, existence, consciousness, and bliss; it is them. It is all the three rolled together as one, the three being inseparable from one another.

As such it is also beyond our concepts, language, and reason. The response to one who might regard this as vague, mystical, or inconsistent is that clarity, transparency, and consistency fail to work as effective criteria at the level of deepest experienceable reality, which is the same as truth or God, especially in its absolute metaphysical aspect.

But the absolute aspect by itself is less consequential than what might be thought from its above description. It does not generate theological dogmatics in Gandhiji as it would in many a religion. Important as it is to postulate the absolute aspect, its impact on actual life is limited. For one thing, there is the implication that its infinite unity pervades all that we perceive and infuses everything under the sun as equal in ultimate terms of being, awareness, and joy.

The one absolute truth appears as the many in the world, translating its unity as equality in the plurality. The finite plurality and diversity of ordinary perception is ultimately an illusion when, and only when, compared with the infinite unity of the absolute aspect of the truth that is God. Intellect is a distinct offspring of the truth, unable to cage the absolute aspect. It is important to accept that essential truth is by its nature inaccessible to linguistic or conceptual articulation. Hence, to dwell upon the absolute aspect intellectually is without use for any practical purposes.

The thing to dwell upon is the relative or existential aspect of truth. This is the crux of the Gandhian concept of truth. The absolute aspect can be detected in Hindu texts. The relative aspect cannot be, being a major Gandhian creation. The absolute aspect in its entirety is beyond us. It would be audacious and even be contradictory to think that a finite being like a human mind can take on the infinite existence, consciousness, and bliss. This does not mean, however, that we are forever estranged from the absolute aspect. The absolute can appear to each of us in a relative way. Each of us, then, needs to focus the concern on the way the absolute appears to oneself in the way one leads one's existence.

Existential Truth

Succinctly speaking, the existential or relative truth which is the way the essential or absolute truth appears to one is always in the form of a course of ethically compelling action.

Truth, for all practical purposes, consists in the vision of an ethically compelling action on the part of one who has compelled oneself ethically. A person who has never compelled oneself ethically and hence has never found any action to be ethically compelling lacks an experiential basis to think about truth in this regard. A truth which does not lead to action is, for efficient human purposes, an empty verbosity. While essential truth is the ultimate ground of all action, existential truth is the best immediate ground of particular action. Existential truth, which is the aspect of truth that matters for the purposes of human interaction, is basically an actional concept.

The upshot is that realizing the truth that is God cannot for a Gandhian consist in anything but the performance of ethically compelling action. For a human the divine is approximated through ethical action. Being able to find ethically compelling action is equivalent to receiving a divine revelation. It is blasphemous or even inconceivable that a true believer who receives a divine revelation to act will not follow it up in action.

But in the Gandhian view, one does not wait for the windfall of revelation. One prepares oneself in a way that will ensure that revelation will be a daily occurrence filling every day of one's life with truthful or ethical action. It is when one's daily wakeful life with every hour, minute, and second in it becomes filled with such action that one gets closer and closer to the realization of the truth that is God. Continuous adherence to the existential truth is for any individual the only way to approximate the essential truth. The latter, which is infinite, can only be approximated by us finite beings. The process to realize it through the existential truth is without end. Hence, the process becomes the substance for all efficient purposes.

Mashruwala defines existential or concrete truth on page 4 in this way, "Whatever action today appears to me to be so proper, just, and right that I ought to do it, would not be ashamed of endorsing and performing it, and would not be able to face the humanity if I do not do it is truth for me. Just that is God's concrete form revealed to me." It is difficult to conceive a more challenging ethic than this. In the least, it implies the need to shed all forms of ethical insensitivity. Besides insensitivity to the demands of ethical action, other impediments to the realization of existential truth are impaired vision and lack of courage.

Derivation of Nonviolence from Truth

The Gandhian way to build sensitivity, vision, and strength needed to realize the truth is as challenging as the Gandhian concept of truth itself. It draws from the nature of the essential truth and its logical implication for the world of human interaction. The essential truth is one and the same in all circumstances. Hence, as the sustainer of human existence as we live it, it equally pervades all that has being for us.

The way it reveals to one as an existential truth is, though, relative to one and is nothing but an infinitesimal fraction of the essential truth which is infinite. While existential is all one has to go by, it could be different in different individuals and one has no way of claiming to be absolutely right for everybody. So, if the way one sees it conflicts with the way someone else sees it, one has no right to impose it on that individual against his or her will. One must change the mind or heart of the individual to one's own vision of the truth.

Because one has no basis to make an exclusive claim to absolute truth, one can never resort to action that will involve a violent imposition of one's view on anyone. Thus, the only way to insist upon one's existential truth, which one must in all circumstances, is through nonviolence. Since the absolute truth is in all and since no one can say he or she has more of it, one must treat everyone to be as much an embodiment of it as oneself. This, however, does not mean that one should not judge any one or cannot evaluate any state of affairs for ethical purposes.

For Gandhiji, what it means is that everyone must oppose untruth as one sees it but one must do it nonviolently. This is how nonviolence is derived from truth. It is important to see that for him it is a rational derivation from truth as conceived and not an independent and separate postulate. Of course, nonviolence is so important a deduction from truth that it merits being regarded as a foundational concept.

To put it differently, the nature of essential or absolute truth as conceived by Gandhiji logically and rationally dictates absolute nonviolence in human affairs. At the same time, revelation of existential or relative truth dictates ethical action to remove untruth. The pursuit of truth, consequently, becomes a persistent nonviolent struggle to remove untruth. One is urged to perceive, find, or identify untruthful states of affairs continuously. Removal of these states of affairs becomes the way truth is pursued and approximated. The removal effort cannot but be nonviolent. Nonviolence thus becomes the foundational means to achieve truth which is the only end of human life having intrinsic worth.

Life of Truth

Because a person engaging in violence acts in contravention to the nature of essential truth, he or she cannot reach the truth even if acting to remove properly perceived existential untruth. Total coherence with respect to both essential and existential truth demands no less than an untiring nonviolent opposition of existential untruth to the end of one's life.

Similarly, nonviolence such as fasting to force someone to follow untruth is inconsistent with the foundational concept of truth and is, therefore, a pursuit of untruth. As soon as a truth-seeker is done with a struggle to remove a specific untruth, he or she will pick up another, and this will go on until the end of the seeker's life. The only way to realize the truth is to spend every minute of one's wakeful life in pursuit of it through action which engages one's consciousness thoroughly. A human becomes one with truth only by remaining absorbed in it through action aimed at preserving it.

No less can be expected of a life of truth. Contrary to some Hindu thought, the life of truth is not an idle or abstract state of reaching a level of consciousness that will end all action. There is no reaching a terminal state of consciousness as long as there remains an untruth to remove in the world. In all likelihood, no truth-seeker is going to reach such a state, for an ethically sensitive seeker will always find some untruth to fight. Therefore, a truth-seeker knows in advance that the pursuit of truth is endless and yet accepts the challenge of making truth as the only goal of life because ethical intuition dictates that nothing but truth has greater intrinsic worth.

Mashruwala's definition of the existential prong of Gandhiji's truth shows the concept of existential truth to be crystal clear for practical purposes. The concept is Gandhiji's original contribution to ethical thought. It guided him in his life, thought, and action in a central and compelling way and it never failed him as far as the need for concrete action was concerned. Conceiving a life of truth as a truth-seeker's ceaseless search for ethically compelling action and undaunted performance of such action in face of any difficulties that may pop up, the concept is self-sufficient, not needing an abstract intellectual prop.

The logical derivation of nonviolence from the interplay of the two prongs of Gandhiji's truth reinforces Gandhiji's frequent assertion that truth was his foundation and nonviolence was the derivation. Being unable to find the concept of truth in a precisely articulated form, some critics have tended to brush this assertion aside as rhetorical rather than substantive. The foregoing articulation makes it clear that Gandhiji meant his statement seriously and with good reason, as can be expected of a good lawyer that he was.

The nearly humiliating challenge to become a truth-seeker pursuing a life of ceaseless action enjoined by extreme ethical sensitivity is hard to exaggerate, especially, in light of the commitment that Gandhiji wants the truth-seeker to make. The commitment is no less than fighting untruth through utterly nonviolent action to the end of one's life in full knowledge of the fact that one will never see the end to the series of ethically compelling actions. Gandhiji did this from dawn to dusk, day in and day out without taking a single day's vacation. Of course, this does not mean that he did not commit any ethical errors. He has himself admitted to committing "Himalayan" blunders.

Importantly, the ethic as conceived promises any individual ceaseless moral growth, which for Gandhiji is the cognate of spiritual growth. The growth is in terms of intuition necessary to grasp ethically compelling actions, facing hardships of remaining nonviolent at all times, ability to adjust with existential truth changing with different situations, and yet being challenged to see it all as the myriad manifestations of the one absolute, transcendental, and immanent essential truth.

CHAPTER THREE

NONVIOLENT WAR ON UNTRUTH

Criticisms, explanations and interpretations of Mahatma Gandhi's thought abound. They often attempt to reduce Gandhiji's ethically uplifting war on untruth to an outcome that barely measures up to the requirements of any of the numerous perspectives infected by what from the Gandhian viewpoint amounts to moral mediocrity typical of a relatively affluent middle class. Since the proliferation of such perspectives is a hallmark of Western modernism, including the newly termed "postmodernism," it is not surprising that the critical explanations are the offspring of Western or West-inspired intellectual effort. The unfortunate result of this effort is myriad interpretations fashioned through misconstruing the Mahatma's thought.

There are attempts to explain the Mahatma as a phenomenon. This is an historical task and we are still too close to the Mahatma's life to explain the phenomenon of the Mahatma. But the unfortunate rush to judge, criticize and explain before having an accurate understanding hurts the integrity of intellectualism.

It is also typical of thinkers who cannot be persuaded that truth, for which the Mahatma stood so resolutely, is not so much to explain and interpret as it is to understand, recognize and act on. Let us try to remedy the situation by putting the Mahatma's thought in its own conceptual terms, albeit conveyed through an intellectual idiom of our times.

The Mahatma's Thought an Enigma to Some Thinkers

One cannot be sure that the Mahatma's intellectual critics have grasped the most important concept in Gandhian thought, namely, that of truth. For, if they did, they would not have paid the unusual attention they have paid to the derivative concept of nonviolence. The Mahatma was clear in his assertion that he found nonviolence in his search for truth and that truth was the end and nonviolence was the means. Apparently, even nonviolence as understood by him cannot be grasped without an understanding of the logically prior goal-concept of truth. But the Mahatma's less than sympathetic detractors, suffering from a self-image of objectivity reinforced by their critical predilection, have variously brushed aside the Mahatma's foundational concept of truth as vague, confused, inconsistent or otherwise ill-conceived.

But the Mahatma's thought hardly ever was enigmatic to be millions of people of India. The Mahatma conveyed it clearly to them in simple language, both spoken and written. More importantly, he conveyed it to them through his actions which were true to his word and hence spoke even louder than his words.

This cannot be said of many a great individual in the history of humanity. The Mahatma spoke and wrote in his native language Gujarati, in his second language English, and in Hindi, the language spoken by more people in India than any other. His English writings were mainly addressed to the minuscule proportion of the people of India who had the luxury of an elite exposure to the Western ways of thinking.

His writings in Gujarati and Hindi were directly addressed to the masses who comprised the true majority of the people in India. The Gujarati and Hindi writings of the Mahatma were translated in other regional languages of India spoken by the rest of the masses. It is well known that the Mahatma was primarily concerned with the toiling masses and did not esteem highly those who live on intellect.

Some who trust no one but themselves to understand any one and are given, as a consequence, to effusive interpretations and causal-looking explanations, have found the Mahatma's thought to be a complex enigma, full of what they want to believe to be inconsistency and disorganization. This is particularly the plight of those Western and Westernized thinkers who take the Mahatma to be nothing but a shrewd and unpredictable politician.

However, other thinkers who were willing to take him at his own word have found little difficulty understanding him. Some of them were those like Netaji Subhash Chandra Bose who believed in an alternative to Gandhian nonviolence and those like Lokamanya Bal Gangadhar Tilak who believed in a more traditional Hindu view than the Mahatma.

Mashruwala's *Quintessence of Gandhi's Thought*

On the other hand, there were intellectuals of the Gandhian ilk who followed the Mahatma's thought closely. They were the Mahatma's close associates working with him in the spiritual communes called Ashrams or in Gandhian academia like the Gujarat Vidyapith or in any of the many aspects of what was known by the Gandhians as "the constructive program."

These intellectuals, working principally through the medium of the Gujarati literature, responded to the people who raised all sorts of intellectual questions and doubts about the Mahatma's thought and program.

The Mahatma himself did not have the time and inclination to respond to these specifically intellectual queries. Both he and the people who made the queries came to trust these Gandhian intellectuals to resolve or otherwise pronounce upon the queries in accordance with the spirit of the Mahatma's thought. Acharya Vinoba Bhave, Maganbhai Desai, Kakasaheb Kalelkar, Ramniklal Modi and Narharibhai Parikh were some of these thinkers who earned this trust from the Mahatma and the people.

But towering among these thinkers was Kishorlal Ghanshyamdas Mashruwala, an independent Gandhian intellectual, who earned the trust as well as respect from all as the foremost commentator on Gandhian thought. He wrote extensively in Gujarati. If his intellectual works were translated in English, much of the Westernized thinkers' self-induced enigma about the Mahatma's thought would dissipate.

These thinkers would also become substantially less inclined to interpret and explain the Mahatma and would properly busy themselves with critically assessing the clear, systematic and orderly commentary of the Mahatma's thought made by Mashruwala.

The book that established Mashruwala's reputation as the foremost commentator of the Mahatma's thought is the celebrated *Gandhi-Vichar-Dohan* or "Quintessence of Gandhi's Thought." It grew out of Mashruwala's assignment to teach the Mahatma's thought in a crash course at a Gandhian school in Mumbai. The Mahatma himself read the manuscript closely, revised it as necessary and approved it as an accurate and authentic articulation of his thinking, commending Mashruwala's extraordinary grasp of his thought.

The systematic style in which Mashruwala expressed the Mahatma's philosophy was also a marvel of terseness and clarity. It remains to date as the most important, authoritative and comprehensive exposition of Gandhiji's philosophy as a whole. Needless to say, Gandhiji did not agree with everything in the early manuscript of the book. He made some changes many of which were minor while some were substantial. He particularly rewrote sections on prayer and spirituality, not being able to agree with Mashruwala's own personal tendencies toward quasi-agnosticism.

The book was first published in 1932; subsequent editions came out in 1935, 1940 and 1963. It reflects the Mahatma's mature thought at the time of his greatest prominence and at the time his most important contribution to civilization was being made. Its importance for accuracy in depicting the Mahatma's thought cannot be exaggerated, for its authority goes unquestioned among Gandhian thinkers and workers who, of all the people, should count heavily in the matter of understanding and articulating Gandhiji's philosophy.

Mashruwala's work, when seriously perused, reveals remarkable cohesiveness of the Mahatma's thought. It also does full justice to the dynamism and flexibility of the Gandhian philosophy. It is divided into fourteen parts each of which is subdivided into smaller sections with each section containing consecutively numbered statements.

The conceptual tightness of the exposition is typical of the systematic way. In which Mashruwala thought. The Mahatma never arrived at such an enunciation or description of his own thought. But he had no problem identifying with it. Some of the Mahatma's followers could have felt that certain of the statements were not encountered in Gandhiji's own writings.

Mashruwala pre-empted these concerns by pointing out that, if the foundational structure of the important Gandhian concepts is properly understood, the whole of Gandhian thought would not be hard to follow. The rather strict follow-up of the logical implications of the foundational principles shows how misplaced is some thinkers; observation of inconsistency and disorganization in Gandhiji's thought.

Need for Conceptual Exposition of Gandhiji's Thought

Once the premature search for a miracle interpretation or explanation is eschewed as an authentic understanding is achieved, a true critique of the Mahatma's philosophy can begin. Much needless though intense energy has been as is still being spent to reach a "correct" interpretation of Gandhiji's thought. The lack of trust in the Mahatma's own words implied in this misconceived intellectual effort does grave injustice to the Mahatma and what he stood for, specifically the principle of truth.

The ignorance of Mashruwala's work has been conducive in allowing this tendentious approach to take roots. Besides that, the Mahatma himself tended to use traditional Sanskrit words in enriched meanings and to employ a multi-layered term when only one of the many meaning-layers was relevant in the context. Masses who use imagination could follow him easily but intellectuals, who need explicit and exact usages to grasp something, had difficulty understanding the Mahatma's "logic" of thought.

What is needed for the benefit of intellectuals looking for such logic is a secure basis of the conceptual drive of the Mahatma's philosophical thinking. With this becoming available, the more promising and potentially productive search for a respectable critique can begin. Rushing to judgmental evaluation before achieving accurate understanding has misled the intellectuals.

More tragically, serious injustice has been done to Gandhiji. I won't say that Gandhiji's thought should not be subjected to fair criticism; what I am saying is that premature criticism of thought assumed to be Gandhiji's and imposed on him needs to stop. Then let the fair criticism ensue on the thought that is properly secured and identified as really belonging to the Mahatma.

It goes without saying that "critiques" attempted through "interpretations" are grossly inadequate, maybe severely handicapped. "Explanations" made in advance of understanding or in prejudgment of the Mahatma's assumed positions are obviously worse.

Since an understanding of the conceptual basis of the Mahatma's philosophy is vitally necessary for the possibility of a legitimate and respectable critique, let us delineate such a basis, along with the intellectual support that can be garnered for it in consonance with the logic of the Mahatma's basic principles. Let us look at significant questions that can be raised against the Mahatma's philosophy of truth. Responses to these questions can then be allowed to form this basis.

Needless to say, the primary source for the conceptual basis in the delineation is Mashruwala's *Quintessence*, although I should not implicate anyone but myself on the adequacy of the responses to be presented in relation to the questions to be raised. I would hold that the responses made are within the logic of the Mahatma's basic principles. I cannot say whether Gandhiji or Mashruwala would have approved the philosophical idiom in which my exposition is expressed.

The idiom used is meant to communicate the Mahatma's thought in a language that is explicit, economical, direct and prosaic enough, hopefully, to suit the intellectuals' needs. My attempt is to fill the lacuna in Gandhian literature I perceive with regard to a philosophically coherent presentation of the Mahatma's foundational thought. That there is a widespread acquiescence among intellectuals that the Mahatma's thought does not admit of such presentation is itself a sufficient indication that the presentation is needed.

A Personal Note

With budding pretensions to intellectuality and scholarship, I did not entertain a great deal of respect for incoherent thought even if it occurred in people regarded as great in terms of spiritual accomplishment. I read and studied these people with a so-called "critical eye" and, applying superficial observations and literal interpretations to their writings in a hasty manner I came to negative judgments about them, mostly in consonance with the intellectual community's view of them.

A change started to occur when I was assigned to teach world religions. I began to develop deeper understanding of the spirituality of the founders of world religions, both Eastern and Western. Teaching a course in Indian philosophy strengthened this trend. Interaction with students also carried this forward, because I could see them too more deeply concerned to understand spirituality in depth. Strangely, teaching my first classes in introduction to philosophy also helped and reinforced this budding appreciation of spirituality wherever I was able to see or find it.

Viewing Richard Attenborough's movie "Gandhi" for the first time opened the floodgates of this flow which was gathering continually for some years. Then as I began to teach Gandhi course, the students' earnest spiritual quest impressed me strongly. Then on, intellectuality started to fade away very fast as my prime tool for approaching the lifeworld and its contents.

By no means it's a revolution, for intellectuality has not died; it still has a respectable place but it does not have its erstwhile top priority. I am still friends with reason, with experience and value its co-equals in my quest for truth and reality. I will recommend this mix, even with the caveat that the proportion of the mix separates people from each other in terms of their view of life. But if all of us admit the mix and respect all the three of its contents, namely reason, experience and value, we have the hopeful promise of a truly beneficial discourse.

As far as it concerns understanding and appreciating the Mahatma's thought, the latter is bound to appear incoherent and even wayward with just nonviolence standing out as a beaming light of beacon there. That is what many an intellectual still gets out of studying Gandhiji. Lightning strikes when one is exposed to his dual concept of truth. Most everything falls in place and things become coherent and the entire edifice begins to look cogent.

Gandhiji insisted that truth was his central concept. Understanding the concept makes it clear why it was so. Its ethic is numbing and overwhelming. I have never encountered a more challenging ethic in my extensive exploration of the entire history of human thought, Eastern and Western. The awe it inspires has a deadening effect on my trained tendency for critical thinking. Eventually, though, I have come to entertain the possibility and desirability of a legitimate critical evaluation of Gandhiji's thought.

Mashruwala says that his work, the *Quintessence of Gandhi's Thought*, is not a distillation of the Mahatma's writings, but a studied attempt to grasp the basic notions and to derive their implications for action in life. It seems this is the only way to understand Mahatma Gandhi if not anyone else. For, if there was one person for whom philosophy and life, or thought and action, became one integrated piece, it was the Mahatma. Any attempt to understand him in terms of concepts not his own is bound to remain an act of cerebral vanity.

Truth as God

The foundational idea of the Mahatma's thought is, of course, truth. But the Mahatma identifies it with God. It is important that God is not identified with truth, because that can only open the field to doctrinal assertions and counter-assertions of myriad types that conflict and confuse.

The Mahatma's God is not a doctrinal concept of an institutionalized religion. For the Mahatma, experiential realization, and not a credulous conceptualization, of God is the fully adequate and the only goal of human life. This is the beginning of his thought in its foundational terms. It is crucial to grasp this, if one is to keep one's head above the vulgar waters of the stereotype that regards the Mahatma as just a complex politician.

Realizing God is, of course, not the same as conceiving God. The truth which is God for the Mahatma has two aspects, one of which is absolute and the other relative. The absolute truth may also be called the essential, transcendental or metaphysical truth and the relative truth the existential, efficient or concrete truth.

The essential truth is always and eternally one and the same. It is one without a second. There is nothing else besides it, for it consists of infinite existence. It *is* all of existence; but it is more. It is infinite consciousness and infinite bliss as well. There is no existence, consciousness and joy beyond or besides it. It does not *have* the three, it *is* the three: existence, consciousness and bliss.

It is all the three rolled together as one, the three being inseparable from one another. As such it is also beyond our concepts, language and reason. If one is inclined to call it mystical, vague or inconsistent, the answer is that transparency, clarity and consistency fail to work as effective criteria at the level of deepest reality which is the same as truth or God, especially in its absolute metaphysical aspect.

But if one does not have the stomach for the absolute aspect of the truth, it may be comforting that all by itself it is less consequential than one might think. This is where Gandhiji departs from the traditional Hindu, particularly Vedantic, thinking which wants to go for it in an exclusive gung-ho manner, forsaking all else in the world. Here he would depart even from Jesus who asked a rich man to give away all his belongings and to follow him. The Mahatma wants to recognize the absolute truth for what it is, that is infinite and all-inclusive existence, consciousness and bliss, and then leave it at that as impossible for human finitude to realize, achieve or otherwise capture in one's consciousness. He won't chase it, beyond acknowledging it and meditating on it to be inspired by it to find and handle the relative and existential aspect of truth.

For Gandhiji the absolute aspect of truth does not generate apodeictic and dogmatic theological assertions as would a concept of God in many institutional religions. Important as it is to postulate the absolute aspect, for the Mahatma its primary impact in actual life is the implication that its infinite unity pervades all that we perceive and infuses everything under the sun as equal in ultimate terms of being, awareness and joy.

The one absolute truth appears as the many in the world, translating its unity as equality in plurality. The finite plurality and diversity we see in front of our eyes is ultimately an illusion when, and only when, compared with the infinite unity of the absolute aspect of the truth that is God. Intellect, which is a distinct offspring of the truth, cannot, through its prideful guiles, cage the absolute aspect. It is important to accept that essential truth is by its nature inaccessible to linguistic or conceptual articulation. Hence, to dwell upon the absolute aspect intellectually is without use for any practical purposes.

Ethically Compelled Action

The thing to dwell upon is the relative or existential aspect of the truth. This is the crux of the Gandhian concept of truth. The absolute aspect can be readily found in the Hindu texts, or even in the texts of other world religions, albeit by a little stretch. Gandhiji's dual concept of truth does not rest with the absolute aspect, only to put it on a pedestal to find an esoteric path to reach it in an ecstatic trance. Gandhiji has a different idea.

For him the absolute aspect in its entirety is beyond us. It would even be contradictory to think that a finite being like a human mind can take on the infinite existence, consciousness and bliss. This does not mean, however, that we are forever estranged from the absolute aspect. The absolute can appear to each of us in a relative way. Each of us, then, needs to focus the concern on the way the absolute appears to oneself in the way one leads one's existence.

To put it succinctly, the existential or relative truth is the way the essential or absolute truth appears to one and is always in the form of a course of ethically compelling action. Truth, for all practical purposes, consists in the vision of an ethically compelling action on the part of one who has compelled oneself ethically. A person who has never compelled oneself ethically and hence has never found any action ethically compelling has no experiential basis to even think about truth in this regard.

Such a person has, at least temporarily, copped out of truth. A truth which does not lead to action is, for efficient human purposes, an empty gesture or pompous verbosity. While essential truth is the ultimate ground of all action, existential truth is the best immediate ground of particular action. Existential truth, which is the aspect of truth that matters for the purposes of human interaction, is basically an actional concept. The failure to realize this has landed many an intellectual into a self-designed snare of misinterpreting the Mahatma's most important concept.

It should be clear now that realizing the truth that is God cannot for a Gandhian consist in anything but performance of ethically compelling action. For a human, the divine is approximated through ethical action. Being able to find ethically compelling action is equivalent to receiving a divine revelation. It is blasphemous or even inconceivable that a true believer who receives a divine revelation to act will not follow it up in action.

But in the Gandhian view, one does not sit around for the windfall of revelation. One prepares oneself in a way that will ensure that revelation will be daily occurrence, filling every day of one's life with every hour, minute and second in it becomes filled with such action that one gets closer and closer to the realization of the truth that is God.

Continuous adherence to the existential truth is for any individual the only way to approximate the essential truth. The latter, which is infinite, can only be approximated by us finite beings. The process to realize it through the existential truth is without end. Hence, the process becomes the substance for all efficient purposes.

This leads to the need to become ethically sensitive in the extreme, shedding the thick desensitizing skin that one usually develops in any society with heavy pressures to survive and prosper. Often, in the face of an ethical need, one fails to see the need to act or rationalizes it away with the help of cleverly fabricated self-serving excuses.

The basis of ethical insensitivity is deep and strong. Contrary to our self-image, the structures that support our insensitivity are well-oiled and established through long-nurtured habit which hardly entertains an inconvenient thought that would compel it towards ethically challenging action. Even so, insensitivity to the demands of ethical action is only one obstacle in the way to the truth. The other and more formidable impediment is impaired vision.

Our ethical vision has become distorted by non-use, misuse or, in some cases, abuse. First of all, we need to restore correct vision, so that we can see the existential truth properly when it is revealed to us. The third obstacle is weakness or lack of courage. Even knowing what is the truth, that is, what needs to be done in order to be truthful, we fail to act because we lack the strength to face the suffering that may be involved in pursuit of the course of action compelled upon us by our ethical sensitivity and vision.

Questions

We have seen earlier how truth is for Mahatma the primary concept, from which nonviolence is derived as the secondary concept. Both truth and nonviolence are foundational concepts, but truth still is primary and nonviolence derivative. We also have seen that intellectuals trying to interpret and explain Gandhiji's thought have derided his concept of truth as murky and devolved upon his concept of nonviolence.

It is interesting to note in this context, that the Mahatma did not find too much difficulty in identifying truth even in difficult situations but has admitted and complained, sort of, that he has struggled with the concept of nonviolence. Many intellectuals are avowed pacifists in rather a dogmatic fashion. They cannot but find this puzzling. For, in their view, Mahatma's truth is murky where he should struggle and nonviolence, being a self-evident dogma in their pacifist credo, should present no struggle.

Given the conceptual edification of Gandhiji's concept of truth in its dual nature of essential and existential modes, Gandhiji's lack of struggle with identifying truth becomes quite understandable. His struggle with nonviolence, on the other hand, is pragmatic. Very often, a seemingly violent act is nonviolent, for example, a surgeon cutting up a patient's stomach to perform appendectomy. Similarly but conversely, an apparent nonviolent act may be violent, such as a nurse purposely not giving an essential medicine to a patient, with an evil intention to harm. Mahatma, therefore, is on solid commonsense grounds in his struggle in securing air-tight criteria for nonviolence.

Still, we do not need to shortchange the intellectual who may not want to let go of the matter without settling legitimate questions. Isn't the concept of truth vague, muddled and inconsistent? It does not ask for any specific action or type of action. What is there to prevent the same person from having different or even conflicting actions appear at different times as concrete revelations of God? What if my actional revelation conflicts with someone else's? How is one to know that a revealed action is ethical, let alone ethically compelling?

These intellectually pertinent questions are indeed relevant. Questions that arise in the logical mode of thinking deserve an answer or at least a response. There is no way to brush them aside and claim some sort of immunity to support unwillingness to respond. But the logic of the Mahatma's concepts does not leave these questions without a response.

To start with, the questions assume that, like an intellectual, the Gandhian truth-seeker will remain self-exiled in an ivory tower, contemplating the revelations, fixing their mutual relationships from a logical point of view. That, however, is not the case.

The Gandhian truth-seeker is a child of concrete action, not of interminable ratiocination. He or she may pray in order to tap the essential truth as an unfailing source of inspiration. But spending endless hours in fixing the logical relationships of revelations would hardly qualify as particularly productive aspect of a life of truth.

On Specificity of Action

But then what is the Gandhian response to the questions? Say a Gandhian truth-seeker, living in any part of the world, wakes up early in the morning, cleans oneself and prays for inspiration. He or she is then ready to go into action. What action does the existential truth dictate?

For one thing, a Gandhian truth-seeker knows one's existential social world extremely well. One knows, for instance, that the family next door has an abused child, a molested step-daughter or a battered wife. Or, the shop next block employs a forced child laborer, sells adulterated food or lends money to desperate neighbors at exploitative rates. Or, the gang of idle youngsters in the street habitually molests pedestrians, especially, women. Or, a bullock is mercilessly beaten by its neurotic owner every day. Or, dozens of children have starved for several days in the central part of the town just a few miles away.

Or, the landlord of the biggest farm in the town gets away paying slave wages to the workers of his farm.

Knowing all this and a lot more if one just goes around and observes one's own community, the question is not figuring out some logical relationships but choosing the best area for action where one can contribute most positively and constructively in a nonviolent way that will ameliorate any of the prevalent unjust situations.

The truth-seeker will probably not decide to spend one's time devising an abstract approach to the problem of world hunger where one is unlikely to get anywhere except publishing an abstruse article in an academic journal of economics which will not provide a loaf of bread to any of the starving millions of the world.

A Gandhian is a person of concrete action who keeps away from temptations of grandiose punditry. As a truth-seeker, one devises an action plan to pursue a constructive program for an actual visible reduction of untruth in one's community. In the Mahatma's view, those who ignore untruth that goes on around themselves can never reach the truth, no matter how high-flying words they use to justify the ignoring or whatever else they do.

Also, a genuine truth-seeker is one who accepts any necessary action that comes along in the journey towards the truth. If it appears that cleaning the street where one lives is urgent in order to prevent a spreading infection and no one else seems ready to do it, nothing would be ethically more compelling than street-cleaning. Street-cleaning, in those circumstances, would be the actional revelation of God's concrete form. No one shying away from that action is going to reach truth.

No action that is truly compelling as the most pressing ethical demand of the time is mean, menial or trivial enough to be ignored. A truth-seeker simply cannot dissuade oneself from acting according to the revelation on the snobbish grounds of false prestige or vain dignity. There are thousands of truthful actions crying out to be performed. Let an individual truth-seeker find one's best avenue of action.

Cerebral curiosity about a principle of action leading to a specific action or type of action is an idle demand with no ethical compulsion in it, especially when thousands of actions that are obviously compelling go begging. The criterion to judge the worth of an intellectual objection, as of any other objection, is whether the objection compels itself ethically.

The objection that the Gandhian concept of existential truth leaves the revealed action vague and unspecified is hardly compelling from the viewpoint of getting the needed actions done. As long as the list of needed actions contains even a few clear and specific actions, no advance need for an abstract clarity or specificity seems even rationally warranted.

To think that a logically well-related network of ideas about clear and specific actions is necessary as a basis for progress in the direction of existential truth seems more far-fetched than the simple Gandhian notion of sensitizing oneself ethically in order to readily find needed actions in one's community and actually doing them.

Human communities are alive and moving. Life is myriad and creates infinite variety of unprecedented situations with plenty of variables playing unpredictably. A demand to specify particular actions or action types in advance shows intellectual frozenness or paralysis. It can lead to dogmatism in the name of reason and is, in addition, patently unrealistic.

A clear and specific action that appears ethically compelling today may not be so tomorrow. Clarity and specificity in advance of all the movements of life and times are too rigid criteria to fit life's demands. Enforced as such, they would ruin life, and the intellectual comfort generated would at best be a pitiful reward for the cost incurred. Clarity and specificity have their proper place in particular situations, where it is obviously beneficial to decide on a clear and specific course of action.

On the Conflict of Actions

There are two conflict questions, one relating to conflicting actions at different times in the same person and the other to conflicting actions of different persons. The Gandhian response to the first question is that a genuine truth-seeker's intuitive perception of the right action continues to grow with time and with ongoing experimentation with truth. The assumption of growth will imply that a later perception is more accurate than a former one. On the other hand, if the truth-seeker has lapsed rather than grown in truth-perception, the reverse might be the case.

Truth-seeking is a personal journey and the truth-seeker is human, likely to err as any human is; one simply has no option but to continue the journey, learning from the lapses and making steady progress thereby. A logician, too, commits fallacies and learns not to commit them again.

The truth-seeker should have faith in oneself that greater experience will be helpful in making one's truth-vision more and more accurate. We are dealing here with life-truth and not a frozen logical formula held at the same temperature artificially for all times to come, regardless of the dynamics of life.

Another way of viewing it would be to say that life has its own dynamic logic, different from the rationalist's logic of eternally frozen consistency. The truth-seeker is not dismayed by the latter and goes on with the journey for truth, not with the goal to fulfill unrealistic demands of an abstract and rigid logic but with a view to learning from the prodding jolts of a dynamic logic of vibrant life.

The response to the second conflict question of interpersonal dissension is that the dissension is only to be expected when we are concerned with using existential and relative truth to reach the transcendental and absolute truth. The latter certainly contains complete unity that resolves all contradictions but, as we have seen, it does not admit of articulation by human reason, which is equipped only to handle the limited affairs of the world of human interaction.

One can even say that the intuitive demand of the logician's inflexible logic is due to the inner perception of the absolute truth, which can only be invariably one and the same. The logician, therefore, knows that such logic is right, but misidentifies the source of the logical truth as somehow belonging to the logic, thereby making the foundation of the rigid logic dogmatic, circular and self-righteous.

The logician's demand for consistency in face of such foundation and in face of his inability to prove the validity of rigid logic independently of that logic itself is indicative of the workings of the inner perception that truth in its ultimate nature can only be invariantly the same in order to be consistent.

But in the dynamic world of finite human affairs this invariance becomes fragmented among plurality of perceivers and a diversity of perspectives. It is then bound to conflict. That, however, is not reason enough to think that my vision of truth is inherently superior to someone else's. The same sun continues to be reflected in every puddle even though the puddles are muddy in varying ways and degrees.

Further, while rigid logic will have to fight this out in an outright destructive way, holding that either my vision is correct or the other person's, but not the both, dynamic logic or existence will allow for individual differences. Since only the transcendental absolute truth is self-same from an eternal perspective, fragmented existential truth cannot but be different, viewed from different individual perspectives.

However, one does not revel in the apparent differences but knows that underneath them all is the absolute transcendental truth which remains the same sustaining the differences like parent does the children with differing tendencies. I will not fight with my sibling truths but try to understand them and live with them by learning from them if I can.

But if I have to make a choice, it will be only for the way I see the truth. Then if I have to fight for my vision of truth, it will not be the other-deprecating nasty fight of a rigid logician, but a nonviolent struggle for a voluntary transformation of the other's vision and heart.

The Gandhian truth-seeker does not engage in a repugnant denunciation of the other who has a conflicting truth-vision, but rather works with him or her as much as one can; however, one does not compromise on fundamental principles as one sees them and will wage a nonviolent struggle to win over the other through transforming his or her heart.

Again, the transformation of the other's heart is not a matter of rhetoric for the truth-seeker; it is a genuine and honest goal for which alone the nonviolent war is waged. In a case where it is mere rhetoric, its character is bound to turn violent when tested under the fire of life's challenges. The truth-seeker will remain stubbornly nonviolent precisely because of one's dual conviction that one has the right vision of truth and that one has no right to violently force it on the other who holds a conflicting vision.

The truth-seeker will not let go of either part of the dual conviction. This is why the Mahatma held that truth and nonviolence are but two sides of the same coin and, while truth can be regarded as the end and nonviolence is the means, the two fundamentally reinforce each other in an inseparable way. With a concept of truth that demands courage of one's conviction at the same time that it respects differences, a staunchly theist

Mahatma was able to work extensively in a harmonious and cooperative way with, among others, an atheistic political leader like Nehru and an agnostic intellectual like Mashruwala.

On Identifying the Ethical

The last question relates with the need to identify a revealed action as ethical or, more hopefully, ethically compelling. How does one know that a revealed action is ethical? For one thing, the Gandhian truth-seeker is involved in the situation which demands action. The truth-seeker is not interested in hypothetical posturing, when a lot needs to be done, if one simply looks around one's community.

There is a definite advantage in being actually involved in a live situation, compared to exercising the intellect in a hypothetical manner. The pressures of the situation coupled with the human individuals and their affairs involved can lead to ideas, options and decisions for constructive and beneficial action which would evade a cozy abstract thinker.

But, beyond the contrast of the concrete and the abstract, a number of items can be listed that would help the Gandhian truth-seeker to weed out incompetent candidates for ethical or truthful action. The first of all is the criterion of nonviolence. If the action revealed to one involves violence in deed, speech or even thought, it would be dismissed as unfit in any situation.

Another criterion to apply would be whether the action serves the interests of those whose legitimate grievances caused the involvement of the truth-seeker in the first place. If the action is timid, convenient or self-reinforcing without helping to redress the grievances in question, a better alternative would be sought. A third criterion would ask if the truth-seeker is willing to risk one's own comfort, security, position or possessions in order to launch the action.

If self-suffering is involved in removing an untruth, the truth-seeker will not skirt it. Out of two actions where one involves and one does not involve self-suffering, the truth-seeker will choose the one that involves suffering, because that will test and try the seeker and lead to stronger will to pursue truth in the future.

Sacrifice of self-interest was for the Mahatma a standing criterion to decide if an action was ethical or ethically compelling. An action that involves such sacrifice is to be regarded as *prima facie* ethical and one would not be easily dissuaded from it without solid considerations to the contrary.

In sum, determining whether an action is ethical is not simply a matter of intellectual judgment, for it importantly includes the training and development of the truth-seeker, who must find the action challenging in actual practice.

Whether an action is ethically compelling rather than just ethical is a matter of the truth-seeker's moral sensitivity. If the sensitivity is well cultivated and expanded, more actions will reveal themselves as compelling. Basically, an action is ethically compelling if the seeker finds that without doing it he or she would not be able to regard oneself as an ethical person seeking truth. Obviously, one has to sensitize oneself ethically to an extent far beyond the commonplace, in order to find a sufficient number of ethically compelling actions to propel oneself towards truth in a sustained manner.

In actual practice, the truth-seeker is an acute observer of what goes on in the community and uses the observations to find situations that demand action. Only those situations are chosen for actional response that the seeker can handle positively and constructively. The seeker does not hanker after drama and is not out to create situations for involvement but only to respond to ones that demand action.

Hence, truth-seeking is usually a matter of responding to contingencies that either exist or arise in one's life. The Mahatma was clear in emphasizing that the seeker is not out to dramatize one's own importance and heroism. He or she is rather to be a servant of the humanity humbly seeking opportunity to pursue truth and remove untruth.

An honest seeker will always find enough to do in any circumstances and must be content to do just that. Truth is not found necessarily in theatrical and extravagant situations that incur a lot of public attention. The seeker readily, gratefully and humbly avails oneself of all and any avenues where a positive contribution can be made, regardless of the social or political limelight.

Given this attitude, the question is not an abstract one of identifying an action as ethical or ethically compelling as much as the concrete one of choosing a situation to respond to and deciding what course of action would best lead to removal of untruth or establishment of truth.

In live situations, the relevant and important question is *what* one ought to do if one is to pursue the truth. The Mahatma has stressed that a truth-seeker who has honestly pursued truth in whatever contingencies and opportunities that have arisen in one's life will have gathered the needed experiential learning to answer this question whenever it arises.

Sitting down in an easy chair to contemplate in advance all the hypothetical situations one might face and then engaging in pedantic casuistry about them is usually not helpful when an actual situation is encountered.

Further, one who has handled small situations as a starter will have experiential and intuitive basis to manage difficult situations. It is very likely that one who is given to dealing with hypothetical situations in the mind alone will not be able to handle them even in one's own predetermined way, because it is one thing to imagine what to do but quite another to be able to do it while standing up to the challenging demands of a live encounter.

The point is not to disparage intellectuality. Intellect is a useful tool and must be used where it is appropriate. But like other tools it too has to be guided in a measured way in order to produce optimum effect. Being overwhelmed by it as the rationalists are can only produce emotional dogmatism that the rationalists are often unable to see that intelligence can be misused, abused and overused as much as any other potentially beneficial instruments. Above all, beneficial applicability of reason needs to be examined with care and not to be exaggerated in a customary and self-righteous manner.

On the other hand, it is often natural to be filled with doubts as to what is ethically compelling in a given situation. The Mahatma once wrote pointedly and poignantly to a friend, "I will give you a talisman. Whenever you are in doubt, or when the self becomes too much with you, try the following expedient: Recall the face of the poorest and the most helpless man whom you have seen and ask yourself, if the step you contemplate is going to be of any use to *him*. Will he be able to gain anything by it? Will it restore him to a control over his own life and destiny? . . . Then you will find your doubts and yourself melting away." (*My Religion,* p. 52.). If this does not quell the doubts and move the heart of an intellectual, probably nothing else will.

Purification of Truth-vision

It was seen earlier that the Gandhian truth-seeker must develop sensitivity, vision and strength with respect to truth. So far we have talked about sensitivity and strength, in the main. The Mahatma has laid great stress on achieving accurate vision of truth. Mere stretch of experience in the open arena of life is not enough for this. Just intellectualizing about hypothetical situations is even less sufficient. What is greatly important, according to the Mahatma, in the order of developing good vision of truth is the purification of ethical intuition.

One is unable to see the truth if the ethical eye is left in the way it is in commonplace life of material pursuits dictated by societal and egoistic demands. The latter usually blur our vision of truth. Our personal interests involve and engage us in a way that will distort the truth in favor of and in consonance with the underlying interests involved in any situation which needs to be judged in the pursuit of truth. No truth-seeker can be successful without making a systematic and disciplined effort to rise above the interests that distort the vision of truth.

The Mahatma would firmly reject intellect's claim to be able to do this, although Western intellectual tradition has spared no words in convincing the world of the claim's self-evident truth. An intellectual's levitations are as likely to distort the vision of truth as anyone else's, for an average person surreptitiously surrenders to one's underlying interests when contemplating a demanding situation.

Barring rare exceptions like Socrates, whom the Mahatma held in high esteem and wrote about, most intellectuals have not set great examples showing that they are better than average in this regard. They have cleverly guised and disguised, advertently or inadvertently, the canons of logic to rationalize and reinforce a vision convenient to their underlying interests. When someone like Schopenhauer exposes them, they lash out against him and call him names, ostensibly in the name of reason, but really in defense of their underlying interests.

The point is that there is no substitute for a studied, deliberate, disciplined and devoted effort to specifically rise above the interests that beguile average humans and distort their vision of truth. We see too often that an employee of a steel factory is not the first one to see that the factory produces significant amount of pollution. An executive of a tobacco company cannot easily see that smoking is as hazardous to health as the surgeon-general says it is. It is hard to persuade a journalist that the right to publish a story can materially conflict with national security. A consumer up to the neck in debt cannot be easily convinced of the need to lower his or her standard of living. A professional philosopher cannot he easily persuaded that being humane, more than being intelligent, is crucial to being civilized.

None of these can claim an accurate vision of truth. An honest and genuine truth-seeker has no alternative but to put truth above any and all interests that can possibly impair the vision of truth. The Mahatma shows an assiduous way to do this systematically and insists that there is no going out of it for a truth-seeker. This, in spite of the intellectualists and even the so-called commonsense oriented cynical egoists excoriating the Gandhian truth-seeker as lacking in wisdom, tact, maturity or sense of reality.

Transcending of Interests

The nearly superhuman task of transcending one's interests in actuality is so supremely challenging that many an idle doubt has been raised regarding its efficacy. But Gandhiji remained undaunted and went on to experiment with his idea of interest-transcending truth with intensity and energy that have hardly been matched in known history.

His life and work are a testimony to an unprecedented endeavor to achieve such truth. It is important to his associates and followers that, even if he did not transcend all his interests, he reached a level of truth-vision that transcended that of most other humans. His uncommon truth-vision also accounts for several of his perceptions of truth which were met with doubt and derision even among those who knew him well, for few of his associates had reached his level of truth-vision.

Most of us, who make abstract intellectual effort at either-or objectivity, nevertheless remain tainted by a thick layer of truth-distorting interests. It does not matter that Gandhiji did not transcend all such interests. This is a matter of degree rather than two-valued logic chopping. That his truth-blurring layer was much thinner than the one worn by most of us is enough to humble us before his achievement rather than make childish efforts to beat him with the revelations of his shortcomings in his own autobiography. Or make infantile attempts to charge him with subjective whims in following his hard-earned truth-vision.

This is as good a place as there is to respond to the logicians' charge of subjective sentimentalism that some logicians might hurl against the Gandhian truth-seeker's way of finding truth. Logic deals with proof and sound reasoning. It has traditionally played this game with a two-valued either-or kind of "logic" where something is either true or false. This is done sitting down in an arm chair, without involving any sort of observation-based humane action that Gandhian truth-seeker focuses on.

So, these theorists would say that the Gandhian truth-seeker is engaged in a personal and subjective quest and has, on that account, no logical merit. It has no objective validity because it does not operate with their sort of conceptual analysis and distinctions of reason which alone, in their view, guarantee objective truth. The Gandhian truth-seeker's perception of truth, hence, is a subjective, personal and sentimental affair, which cannot even begin to match their purely objective logical methodology.

Cynical intellectual theorists charging sentimentalism on "do-gooders" would hate to have tables turned on them. For, they dislike being dragged into matching the Mahatma's interest-transcending effort. They have no stomach for even a very watered-down hemlock! They would hope that accusing Gandhiji of the fallacy of subjective sentimentalism would obviate the need to match his effort in real life.

The hope would have a chance if the Mahatma was another academic theorist who could be beaten with the scepter of a logical fallacy which makes its limited sense in the constricted world of logical truth conceived as an objective commodity uninvolved in human affairs. But the Mahatma's truth is conceived as existentially human to start with. In his view, a concept of truth uninvolved in human affairs is a piece of pointless pedantry. Hence, far from beating a Gandhian truth-seeker, the scepter would rather boomerang and beat its holder.

It is important to keep in mind that the Mahatma's truth is viewed as human and humane action, making the Mahatma an actional and not an intellectual casuist or a truth-evaluator. In order to meet the challenge of the Mahatma's actional truth, intellectual theory of truth or knowledge will have to achieve a radically critical self-assessment. With all its action restricted to abstract theorizing, it cuts an extremely poor shape for itself, viewed from the perspective of actional truth-seeking.

As indicated, the Mahatma's interest-transcending effort was systematic and disciplined. Progress in the direction of such radically challenging transcendence is not achieved as a windfall. A determined endeavor with nearly superhuman perseverance is called for to make a dent. But in the Mahatma's view, any human is inherently capable of it and it is a disservice to dissuade any individual from making the effort. To say the least, the discouraging attitude found in many intellectually locked-down thinkers is, from the Gandhian viewpoint, as unfortunate as it is negative in helping the humanity make progress towards actional truth which stands for justice and well-being for all, particularly the oppressed and exploited.

The Means of Transcendence

Nonviolence in thought, speech and deed is an obvious ingredient in the transcending effort. With it, the effort's goal of purifying the truth-vision draws closer. It should be clarified that for the Mahatma the limited and negative-looking word "nonviolence" carries an extensive meaning where the adherent of nonviolence becomes one with the attitude of not hurting any living beings and dedicates oneself totally to their good to the extent of risking one's own comforts, interests and security. In other words, his nonviolence is the same as what many would call an unflinching practice of unconditional love.

Not even a trace of hatred for anyone is to be left in the mind of the genuine observant of nonviolence. It is clear that, if and when an observant gets close to perfecting such attitude of total love, one gets close to truth in its absolute aspect too, for the latter is defined as one and the same existence, awareness and bliss that dwells equally in all. The attitude of respecting all and treating each as one's own self is to be expected of one who has realized the truth in its absolute aspect. Perfection of nonviolence as an observance is, therefore, itself an approximation to the truth.

That the nature of absolute truth as conceived dictates this attitude shows how truth and nonviolence go together with each other and strengthen the observant through their joint impact. Truth as an observance also includes for Gandhiji the gross popular meaning of speaking the truth at all costs. The popular meaning is not obviated by the special extended meaning in which Gandhiji uses the word "truth." It is rather included in the larger composite meaning, which mainly denotes the absolute and relative aspects of truth.

One who is not committed to speaking the truth without even a thought to suppressing or distorting it ever for any selfish purpose cannot, of course, be said to be moving towards the truth in its wider meaning. Such a person is clearly involved in cheating, which contradicts both the unity of the absolute aspect of truth and the attitude of total nonviolence implied by it. That truth is a composite concept for Gandhiji does not at all imply that there is any looseness in it; on the contrary, the different aspects of the composite are thus seen to be coherently integrated with each other.

CHAPTER FOUR

OTHER RESOLVES

Logically, truth and nonviolence should, therefore, be a perfect pair of observances which, through their implications and ramifications, would cover all other traits that might also help one move towards the ultimate goal of realization of the truth. However, for the sake of concrete and specific guidance in life, the Mahatma brings out in specific bold relief the need to observe some of the important traits that aid the interest-transcending effort of the truth-seeker.

Gandhiji calls them and lists them as observances or resolves. Besides truth and nonviolence, others in the list include directed conduct, food regulation, non-stealing, non-hoarding, self-reliance including physical labor, community products, fearlessness, removal of untouchability or prejudice and equal respect for all religions. A famous Gujarati quartet enjoins that eleven observances should be regarded as absolute resolves to be practiced all the time and with firmness and humility.

For the Mahatma, truth can be regarded as the leading concept from which other observances can be seen to follow like corollaries. Alternatively, one can regard truth and nonviolence as the leading pair of concepts from which the others can be derived. Of course, more specific resolves can be added, although Gandhiji would not be comfortable losing any from the above list.

What is important for understanding is that the logic of the concepts of truth and nonviolence automatically leads to these other resolves, which then provide the outline of the celebrated Gandhian lifestyle. The resolves provide a coherent philosophy of living and their diligent and devoted pursuit takes the truth-seeker further towards developing ethical sensitivity, truth-vision and spiritual strength to withstand and overcome the inevitable obstacles in the path leading to the realization of truth.

The logical coherence of the resolves with the central concept of truth can be indicated without going into the particularities of each resolve. The intimate relationship of truth with nonviolence has already been seen. Directed conduct means controlling the temptations that distract from the truth. If truth is going to be the sole goal, everything else must either give way to truth or merge itself in the pursuit of truth. Undeterred by temptations and undelayed by distractions, the seeker can devote all energies to the task of disciplining oneself for the long journey toward the truth. The most controversial among the ingredients of directed conduct mentioned by the Mahatma are the control of the sexual drive and the control of the palate.

Some critics assert that in his stringent insistence on these aspects, the Mahatma was being oblivious to human nature, which incorporates sex and appetite as its strongest drives. But they miss the point that the Gandhian goal is not utmost ventilation of biological drives but realization of truth conceived as ceaseless performance of ethically compelling actions. It is hard to connect egoistic satisfaction of biological drives with ethically compelling action oriented through total involvement in selfless public service.

There is no need to examine extensively the crude and self-serving view that sex and appetite should not be shunned because they are "natural," for the view has to define "natural" conveniently to include licentious behavior, while excluding temperance and moderation. Even animals fall far short of what the advocates of "natural" ventilation of sexual drive desire.

Disciplining oneself and organizing one's efforts toward realization of truth is for the Mahatma the primary element of directed conduct. It is from this that the need to control the sexual drive and the palate emerges, for sex and appetite are obviously two of the most time-devouring and energy-consuming distractions in the path of truth. A wholehearted devotion to truth does not seem possible for a weakling who becomes a slave to them.

Nevertheless, some critics have vulgarized this aspect of the Mahatma's thought by making it look like the Mahatma's idiosyncrasy, to be "explained" through a Freudian or similar presumptuous perspective that reinforces moral mediocrity rather than uplifts from it. They should rather show how a single-minded pursuit of truth would be possible in face of any such tempting distractions. If anything, the Mahatma here is trying to propound an extremely stringent and demanding altruistic ethic as an all-consuming religion or spirituality. To dilute its rigor by cowering to base pedestrian passions has no inherent logical strength. To bring in Freud, who is not noted as a great exemplar of ethics or spirituality, as support is juvenile self-serving and pandering to the base instincts of humanity.

And what are the alternatives? They might include advocating a non-truth goal or a composite goal divided among truth and non-truth. But such advocacy would mean devising and defending an alternative philosophy of life and facing the Gandhian philosophy on its own comparative merits without taking cheap-shots in the name of human nature or some other convenient, ill-defined and presumptuous notion such as "natural." Bring it on and see how it looks in face of Gandhism! In place of wholesome food for the soul, we will get some adulterated beverage for the body.

In the matter of controlling the sex drive, Gandhiji is in the good company of many a spiritual tradition the world over and over the history of humanity. Jesus, Socrates, the Buddha, Mahavira among personages and all types of monastic orders through the history of the world have emphasized the sex drive being a major obstacle in pursuing spiritual goals. True, they also have noted how hard it is to overcome this obstacle. But succumbing to it with tail between the legs is not Gandhiji's recipe.

On the one hand, Western psychology, barring some enlightened figures like Jung and Maslow, places "normalcy," a euphemism for conformist mediocrity, on top of its goal-range. On the other hand, its vocational arm of psychiatry has a hard time identifying perfectly "normal" human beings. So, strangely, normalcy which should be abounding in all societies everywhere and all the time, ends up being a rare commodity so that psychiatry can have a ready and full supply of potential patients. Abnormal is the normal!

Strangely and with a straight face, this type of prevalent Western psychology seeks to "explain" all deviation from its "normal." It very conveniently, and rather very ignorantly from the moral-spiritual perspective, conflates as "abnormal" those who surrender to their animal nature, becoming licentious, promiscuous and perverse and, at the other end, those who, through self-directed disciplined course of action, rise above the normal and are restrained, abstinent and a cut above the base, achieving superconscious levels of spirituality.

These psychologists' vocational self-interest clearly guides their own philosophy of mind. They have no logical *locus standi* to lecture any spiritually advanced persons to bring them down to their mediocrity-worshipping normalcy and, on top, "explaining" their behavior as if they are the same as psychotics. As Samuel Goldwyn said, anyone who wants to be a psychologist should have his head examined!

Let us have the normalcy psychologist face the Gandhian straight out, whose questions are these to the psychologist who is criticizing Gandhiji's making of truth and nonviolence into religion, sort of: Does your normalcy ever include participating in a societal injustice to any individual or group? Or, does it ever imply ignoring such injustice? Examples of injustice would be like inequality of women, child labor, oppression of minorities. Horror or horrors: Does normalcy ever promote injustice?

If the psychologist's much-touted normalcy does not involve itself in any way with a societal injustice of any kind, one would like to know exactly how and applying what criteria does it filter out instances of injustice. And after noticing injustice, does the largely conformist normalcy oppose it in any way, just as the Gandhian does? Or, would the psychologist like to play a logician charging the Gandhian of *ad hominem* questioning? But the psychologist started out by doing *ad hominem* criticism of the Gandhian in the first place!

There are questions of professional ethics where, too, this normalcy may be found wanting. Apparently, psychologists will have to step out of their normalcy box to respond to the Gandhian's ethics questions in a morally exculpatory way. Where are they going to pull their ethics from to show their moral invulnerability? Or, how at all do they avoid moral vulnerability?

Gandhian is not playing holier-than-thou in this context; for he or she is simply asking if the psychologists have any moral scruples at all as part of their harboring of normalcy. They cannot escape their self-created trap by claiming arbitrary immunity from ethics or pleading that they are being asked *ad hominem* questions, for they themselves have undertaken to criticize Gandhism *ad hominem* as a starter.

We are not even touching, in this context, the multiple sources of liability and vulnerability faced by Freudian and other paradigms of Western psychology, compared to Eastern forms such as Yoga psychology, Abhidharma psychology or Vedantic psychology. In philosophy of psychology or philosophy of mind, several issues are unresolved. Is the so-called normalcy relative to a culture? To history? To a geographic region? Is it an average or mean of behavior determined quantitatively? Or is it fixed arbitrarily, as what some white men have decided at a particular time in history? What are its ingredients and how are they determined and formulated?

Freud's wife is said to have thought that her husband's theory had something to do with pornography. Well, Freud's analytic psychology had several rivals, in Jung and others. The whole discipline of psychology, after its separation from philosophy by William James at the turn of the twentieth century, suffers from multiple paradigms like Freudianism, behaviorism, phenomenology and so on. Its introspectivism may have been killed by its modern versions, but can the latter be conceived without introspective speculation of some kind? This internal fracture is in itself an indication of serious theoretic schizophrenia, to say the least.

Back to Gandhism, like nonviolence, the concept of non-stealing also is widely inclusive. It means not using, receiving or possessing anything that one does not obviously and absolutely need. This, of course, dictates utter simplicity and non-possessiveness, which were the hallmarks of the Gandhian lifestyle. Not rising to their level of mediocrity and capitalist consumption and greed, this too is apt to attract a high-sounding label of a mental or behavioral disorder from the psychologists, so they can "diagnose" and "cure" it.

And if they do not have that much audacity, they can at least call it an idiosyncrasy or an equivalent aberration and "explain" it away. Professional name-calling! Giving things professional-looking labels and then assuming that such name-calling is a rational explanation of their occurrence!

Let us grant nobility to somebody who brings someone from a level lower than yours to your own level, even for money. But, what do you call someone who, for money, wants to bring someone at a higher level down to your level? Of course, for psychologists the highest level anyone can achieve is never anything better or higher than "normal." And, since nobody is normal, to become normal would be an overachievement.

Is it strange that psychologists as a group are usually, and with a little disdain, regarded as a little abnormal, if not worse, by the outside society of normal people? It is not unusual to see medical practitioners outside the field of psychology referring to their psychiatry colleagues as little off. Do we need another level of meta-psychiatry to help bring these normally abnormal psychiatrists to normalcy?!

The resolve or vow of non-hoarding, for Gandhiji, similar to that of non-stealing, means not keeping anything beyond immediate needs. Non-stealing and non-hoarding together constitute the property aspect of the interest-transcending effort. They involve a drastic reduction of property interests on the part of a truth-seeker. Having less interests means having to transcend less interests. Not having a lot of interests to distort one's truth-vision is a distinct step in the direction of removing obstacles from the path of truth-perceiving.

Also, the reduction of property interests translates into more time for truth-seeking, as it releases time that would otherwise have to be spent for the maintenance and upkeep of the property interests. As seen earlier, of course, owning or possessing a property, such as a bank account or corporate shares, makes one to defend and justify bank or corporate misbehavior in self-defense, which is a gross distortion of truth.

The drastic reduction of property interests recommended by the Mahatma involves voluntary acceptance of a radically lowered standard of living. It does not depend on the society for the upkeep of a high standard of living. This is underscored by the vow of self-reliance, which insures independence from societal pressures, so that a dependence on the society does not handicap the pursuit of truth or necessitate caving in to an untruth in the society.

Self-reliance also contributes to freedom in its most dignified sense, where an individual does not have to compromise the fairness of one's judgment for the sake of maintaining a line of social credit. Looking after one's basic needs through physical labor keeps one close to the nature and to the millions of toiling masses of humanity. This closeness is an element in the closeness to the truth itself. Physical activity involved making for positive health effects is a bonus!

Self-reliance does not mean an isolationism of an egoist. The Gandhian truth-seeker is deeply involved in community affairs and vigilant observation. Love of all starts with the love of neighbor. Loving the neighbor involves commitment to using products made indigenously by the community of neighbors.

This does not mean rejecting or hating products manufactured outside the community. If members of all communities make such commitment, every community would become a well-knit and largely self-reliant group, where members relate with each other on a day-to-day, face-to-face, interactive and cooperative basis, leading to greater harmony, cohesion and unity. Truth, being ultimately a unity, is close to unitive harmony in community. It is relevant to remember in this context the Mahatma's Ruskin-inspired maxim that no one can be truly happy if anyone in the community is unhappy.

The Gandhian truth-seeker must conquer fear. Fear can strike from within and from without. Fear from within indicates lack of self-confidence and of faith in truth. Belief in truth as God can help quell self-doubts and strengthen faith. The Mahatma resorted to both individual and mass prayers to seek inspiration and to cleanse truth-vision. Other means include fasting for self-purification.

Fear from external sources indicates giving in to forces of untruth. If one is steadfast on truth as revealed to oneself from the deepest self and has made sure that it is not a cover for self-interest, there will be nothing at all to fear from forces stacked against it. The truth-seeker will gladly lay down one's life fearlessly fighting for the truth as he or she sees it.

The Mahatma made the removal of untouchability into an observance. This was a response to the evil of untouchability prevalent in Gandhiji's own religion of Hinduism. Untouchability in Hinduism is a gross, explicit and repugnant form of prejudice against an entire group. But prejudice in more or less virulent form exists in all societies.

In the West, it is more obvious in the way racial and ethnic minorities, and even the homeless, are treated. Hence, the vow against untouchability in its globally extended form should be regarded as a vow against prejudice, *mutatis mutandis.* A truth-seeker will make keen observation to detect prejudice in one's community and then launch an action program to combat it through nonviolent means. Removal of prejudice almost universally appears ethically compelling, making it unnecessary to devise an elaborate support to show its coherence with the concept of existential truth.

Most religions in their formative stages succeed in uniting their people under a concept of divinity. In their subsequent institutionalized stages, however, many break into divisive sects and denominations, let alone cults, undoing the message of unity and harmony exemplified by their original forms.

The power of religion to unite and, therefore, to help people move closer to the essential truth by promoting a life of existential truth does not need historical proof. What needs to be fought is the divisive tendencies that foster untruth in the form of narrowly conceived sects that dish out salvation and other goodies to select groups and individuals who meet certain credal conditions. The primacy of the ethical is replaced by that of a credal dogma.

This evil can be removed from the world phenomenon of religion if an equal respect for the positive, that is, unitive and ethical aspects of all religions is fostered in a deliberate manner. Cooperation from different religions is necessary, but the truth-seeker of the Gandhian persuasion does not sit around till the desired cooperation shows up.

A distinct advantage of Gandhian truth-seeking is that any and every individual can plunge and absorb oneself into the seeking without having to wait for anyone or anything to come around in a preferential way. Equal respect for all forms of spirituality that promote ethical life can be practiced by the truth-seeker without waiting for others to do so. The Mahatma enjoins it as one of the observances following from his concept of truth. Further, in his view, the concepts of divinity central to the apparently different religions are close to his concept of essential truth. This is fitting icing on the cake of his truth.

The Label of Asceticism

It should be clear that the Mahatma's list of observances for the truth-seekers in the spiritual communes he established was in strict consonance with his central concept of truth. The observances were conceived and defined to serve truth-seeking by providing a means of transcending self-interests that impair the truth-vision.

They were meant to strengthen the truth-seeker's faith in truth. They inculcated determination to follow the dictates of truth at all costs. Their assiduous practice in the mutually supportive atmosphere of the *ashram* or commune was encouraged as a means to promote a life of truth in the service of community. The ethically charged atmosphere often led to the development of high moral sensitivity in the members, a necessary ingredient in the single-minded pursuit of existential truth.

Despite the mutual cohesiveness of the observances together with their coherence with the central concept of truth, the label of asceticism has been pasted on the *ashram* lifestyle by adversely disposed thinkers. The label does little to elucidate the conceptual underpinnings of the life of truth. It conjures up false images of doctrinal masochism pursued with dogmatic fervor.

The label fails to consider the experiential basis of the observances and the sharing of the experiences that the Mahatma had with other experiential truth-seekers. It ignores the debates and discussions that went on regarding the details and enforcement of the observances. Stalwart Gandhians like Kakasaheb Kalelkar, Mahadev Desai, Ravishankar Maharaj, Vinoba Bhave, Jugatram Dave, Chandrashankar Shukla and Maganbhai Desai, not to speak of Kishorlal Mashruwala, participated actively in the discussions and development under the painstaking leadership of the Mahatma whom they lovingly called "Bapu" or father.

Questions were directed to the Mahatma by the *ashram* members on fine points of observances in the way they were directed to the Buddha by the monks in his monasteries twenty-five centuries ago. They made the Mahatma think and rethink deeply.

For those who really followed the Mahatma and grasped the concepts of truth and nonviolence in their true depth and committed themselves to them with their heart, life was never the same. Their life not only enriched the community; it still stands as an example to inspire many. It shows clearly that the life of truth is not a bed of roses in an intellectual utopia.

Truth was something for those seekers to bring about in their lives. It was not an idle ideology devised with high hopes, asserted in endless debates and yet followed by little action. The so-called asceticism of the Gandhians meant hard work and exemplary self-suffering in the service of humanity.

Criticism based on ideological posturing from an adverse hypothesis without any support of experience or experimentation with socio-ethical action, expectably, is not worth serious attention from the Gandhian viewpoint.

The strict adherence to the observances on the part of many Gandhian truth-seekers provided them with a fountain of energy that stood by them even in their most trying times. From the Gandhian perspective, pejorative labeling is to be studiedly disregarded without response in kind, for engaging in such response wastes valuable time and energy that is better used in building the clear vision of truth.

The most important point is that the difficult practices that look no more than idiosyncratic asceticism to curious and bookish intellectualizers were instrumental in the truth-vision of the practitioners. The latter-day corruption of the politicians who conveniently professed to be Gandhians shows clearly that those who did not have adequate foundation in the observances failed miserably in perceiving the truth, let alone following it up with grit and determination.

The imposition of a measure of discipline on oneself was a part and parcel of truth-seeking for the Mahatma. No truth is ever achieved and sustained without self-discipline. Greater the discipline, greater the results. It is a disservice to label the ever-needed self-discipline as a doctrine of asceticism, for it is no way to immunize oneself from having to go through what one needs to in order to reach truth.

Truth-hating as an Intellectual Fashion

Since Nietzsche declared that God was dead, vocal intellectual forces have cropped up that love to denigrate truth as well. Analytic philosophers have variously tried to reduce truth to a manner of speaking about dead facts, making it look as trivial as they could, with a so-called no-truth theory of truth. Their long-faced dissertations on trivialized truth evince a self-contradictory way of pursuing truth. It is hard to understand what they are doing if not pursuing truth in their own self-discrepant way.

At least, they are not pursuing untruth! It is hard to see how they can be taken seriously except within a self-constituted group of fellow practitioners. There has been precious little involvement in the plight of the toiling and suffering masses of the world on the part of the post-imperialist generations of intellectuals. In view of this, the lack of celebration they have endured is of their own making.

Existentialist philosophers and their post-modern generations have dealt with existential states of affairs without, for the large part, committing themselves to specific ethical values except turning human individuality into a vanity fair. They have tended to dramatize the relatively insignificant pursuits and shortcomings of the modern-day middle-class individuals. The middle-class morality that cannot find a way to uplift itself dramatizes its misgivings and receives some response from young readers. Farther than creating a terminology to depict what they call existence, the existentialist thinkers have trapped themselves into a no-action alley.

In abstract terms, the Mahatma's work on truth can be compared with the theistic existentialists' work on God and the atheistic existentialists' work on individual freedom. But the eye-catching difference is that both types of existentialism avoid concrete problems of the world facing millions who are less well off than the middle class. Living and developing in the existential world of the interpersonal ethics like the Gandhians did receives scant attention, excepting rare cases like Tolstoy.

Thus, from the Gandhian viewpoint, existentialist work cannot be regarded as much more than a terminological ventilation of the guilty feelings of the middle class. Actions speak much more than words. Dramatization of the relatively trivial is scarcely a way to promote truth of a serious kind. It is no wonder that the existentialists, along with their sequel, postmodernism, trivialize or denigrate truth as well, calling it names like logocentrism, bad faith, inauthentic, privileged, what not. Where is the action, other than sloganeering?

Truth-seeking demands rising above entrenched self-interests and asks for extreme courage to stand up to maddening difficulties. Wallowing in the trivial and blowing it out of proportion is a middle-class luxury that can amuse but not help the masses of the world. It is also a mockery of the plight of the large underprivileged masses of humanity, if one simply thinks how the existential plight of these millions is callously ignored in the exuberant depiction of the existential problems of the middle class.

For instance, the long-standing existentialist concern about how an individual is to find or create meaning in life without belief in a personal God who was custom-made in the image of the Western civilization is indicative of the hold of the middle-class perspective in contemporary West.

Even a little of Gandhian discipline and risk-taking experimentation with truth can cure most of the self-inflicted woes of the middle class. But it may jeopardize the profession of existential psychiatry. A compassionate ethical concern for the suffering masses who are left to be the lonely subjects of do-gooders would go a long way in establishing existentialism as a truly humanitarian philosophy.

But the existentialists with such concern have tended to take an easy ideological route toward Marxism of one kind or another. The toiling yet seriously deprived masses continue to be the unhelped subjects of capitalist do-gooders and Marxist ideologues.

Gandhian truth that takes them to its heart is wished out of existence by both the analytic and the continental philosophers. If the moral stagnation of its huge middle class is all that the Western civilization has to offer to these masses, Western thought will cut a sorry figure for itself in the future history of humanity, at least from the Gandhian perspective.

What Gandhian philosophy of truth-seeking action provides is a concrete integration of theory and practice, idea and action, absolute and relative, essential and existential, experimentation and intuition, moral upliftment and socio-economic betterment. It does not let one swerve from the ethical concerns to lapse into doctrinal formulations of the theologians or ideological pronouncements of the intellectuals.

If it seems to carry a heavy spiritual coloring as in the personal belief-world of the Mahatma, not a whole lot can be made out of it to drag it down into dust. The Mahatma was an indefatigable reformist and yet he did not impose his personal belief-world on his associates and willingly and gladly worked shoulder to shoulder with secular atheists and conservative believers alike. That is the spirit of truth-seeking which he admonished the humanity to take up as its historically most challenging and constructive task.

The Mahatma's Personal Spirituality

The Mahatma's central philosophy of truth needs to be taken apart and understood by itself as the foundation on which various structures can be built. This is a most important requirement for understanding him accurately and in depth. With the exposition of the foundations of his philosophy, it is hoped that this requirement is met. With its help the structures and their variety will be put into their auxiliary place and will not land one into needless puzzlement.

Among the structures built upon the foundation is the Mahatma's own belief-world. This world was his spiritual home. His statements made from the home should be taken in their proper context and should not be hastily contrasted with his out-of-home statements. Such literalist contrasting would be pedantic and myopic, hurting the integrity of intellectual scholarship.

Though for the Mahatma as a deeply spiritual person the two types of statement are rolled into a single fabric of belief, they ought to be carefully segregated, if one is to understand his conceptual foundation, which he recommended to all as distinguished from his personal spirituality where he made his home. One who fails to make this important distinction between in-home and out-of-home aspects needs only to consider the last observance in his list the Mahatma enjoined on all, namely, equal respect for all forms of spirituality.

The Mahatma's personal experience was profound and had a deep impact on his life. It made it impossible for him to entertain atheistic alternatives. This, though, never gave him difficulties in appreciating the perspective of atheists who were deeply ethical and actively humanitarian. Although his spiritual experience was real for him, he regarded it only as the way the absolute truth revealed itself to him in a relative personal form. This is how he avoided the temptation to turn his personal experience into a religion of his own with all the trappings of an institutionalized form to be propagated as the absolute truth. Put in his own terms, he consciously avoided the trap of conceiving God as truth.

But he never quit identifying truth with God. With this identification, the structure of his home started to be raised from the foundation. The Mahatma went on to call his God by the name Rama. In Hinduism, the Mahatma's native religion, Rama is the human form in which the divine incarnated to illustrate the life of truth, among other things.

The exemplification of the life of truth gripped the Mahatma more than other aspects of Rama. Since his childhood Gandhiji enthroned Rama in his heart as the ruler of his spiritual self. It is a fact that his spiritual self, seeking nothing but truth, consumed all his mature energies. Rama was the personification of the absolute truth for him. This does not mean that everyone should have a personification of one's own, let alone have Rama as the only possible personification. But Rama is the form in which the Mahatma personalized the absolute truth.

Time and again, Bapu or father of the Indian nation would stretch himself out into the lap of Rama, anxiously awaiting an inspirational revelation of what he ought to do in scores of historically crucial situations in his life of many trials, exercising leadership as a trustee of millions of people who laid their trust in him.

Bapu's own testimony is that his spiritual father never failed him. He could find his Rama in his heart at a moment's notice, to protect him from untruth and to fill his way to truth with difficulties, only to strengthen him and bless him with never-failing vision of existential truth. He found his faith growing without stopping, to the extent that even the assassin's bullets that pierced his heart could not make him forget Rama, for he died speaking the name Rama that always gave his heart peace.

Constructive Program and Truth-persistence

Gandhiji did not build his spiritual home as the only structure on his foundational philosophy of truth. The *ashram* lifestyle of keeping observances can be regarded as an adjoining non-home structure resting on the same foundation. The disciplined maintenance of the observances is the way any individual can lead a life of truth for oneself and make continuous progress toward realizing the truth in one's life.

Joining an *ashram* or commune is greatly supportive of the truth-seeking effort but is not a requirement for it. Besides the observance structure of the communal life of the commune, there were socio-economic structures as well as socio-political structures that the Mahatma built upon the foundation of truth and nonviolence. The most notable among the socio-economic structures was the action design he called "constructive program" and the most celebrated among the socio-political structures was the strategy he called *satyagraha* or "truth-persistence."

Many have sought to opine on the value of the constructive program and truth-persistence by looking at them in parts isolated from their coherent links with the foundational concepts of truth and nonviolence as the Mahatma understood them. Distortions and misjudgments, not to speak of oblique self-reinforcement of one's own value agenda, have been the result of this misdirected effort. The way to understand these two important features of Gandhiji's thought is to see them as two of the important structures that the Mahatma built upon the foundation of truth and nonviolence.

The items receiving significant attention in the constructive program included communal unity, removal of untouchability, liquor prohibition, handspun clothing, development of cottage industries, rural cleanliness, basic education, adult learning, uplift of women, health care, regional languages, national language, economic equality, uplift of farmers, laborers, ethnic groups, the sick and the students.

It is obvious that his observant eye examined the prevalent state of the people in the Indian society with thorough care in order to identify the particular points of untruth suffered by the people. Constructive program primarily means identifying the specific issues of untruth in one's society and quietly but doggedly working to remove them, taking unilateral actions or making solitary moves, when necessary, exemplifying one's irreducible commitment.

The actions and the. Moves have to fit the Mahatma's sweeping concept of nonviolence, with no trace of hatred toward the perpetrators of the untruth in question. Raising of awareness and mobilization of resources would be essential but mere propaganda and sloganeering would be avoided. The point is to have a program of action that will construct or reconstruct truth from the ashes of untruth.

Often, the political glare of truth-persistence has distracted thinkers from seeing the quiet but crucial place of the constructive program in Gandhiji's thought. A life dedicated to constructive program is in no way less important than a dramatic display of media-exciting action in pursuit of a cause of truth-persistence. Such a life is itself a spiritual pursuit of truth that is God.

Moreover, such a life is the best and necessary preparation for the demands of a cause of truth-persistence as long as such a cause has not arisen or dawned upon the truth-seeker with a clear impact. These demands are going to be stringent. One is advised to pursue and devote oneself to constructive program, if one is not yet ready to meet them. Action and experience in constructive program can provide the strength to meet the demands of truth-persistence.

It is the Mahatma's various dramatic undertakings in pursuit of truth-persistence that have earned him the status of a super-celebrity. Gradualistic though radical social reform intended by the constructive program can consume the truth-seeker's life completely. But occasions can arise when the seeker may decide to quit the relative quietude of the constructive program and launch a dramatic nonviolent encounter with untruth that can attract the attention of everybody around.

These occasions can be internal when, for example, the seeker's attention is directed to a glaring injustice that was hitherto neglected. Or they can be external when a glaring case of injustice precipitously arises or builds itself to the point where it demands the involvement of the seeker.

For the Mahatma, two most notable cases in his own life were his experience of racial prejudice in South Africa and the injustice inherent in the foreign rule of India. The first led gradually to the development of truth-persistence as the most potent weapon in the arsenal of the nonviolent seeker of truth.

The second led to protracted development of that weapon against the British rule of India.

The deployment of the weapon of truth-persistence becomes necessary when an obviously hurtful case of injustice cannot be resolved through communication and persuasion. The Mahatma observed that when this happens within a family, one resorts to a rather dramatic self-suffering in order to change the heart of the unjust person.

Because love happens to tie the family together, there is no question of harming the wrong-doer. Love for the wrong-doer coupled with extreme concern for truth leads to inflicting of visible and drastic suffering on oneself to draw the attention and thought of the wrong-doer to the situation. Often, the wrong-doer is alarmed by the self-suffering of the wronged and is able to recognize the unjust nature of his or her actions. This leads to a transformation of heart and to a voluntary but thorough change in behavior, ultimately greatly strengthening the love that already existed between the parties.

The Mahatma sought to apply this very effective familial practice to social situations of injustice. The self-suffering took the form of fasting, noncooperation, civil disobedience, courting of jail and so on. Such dramatic action at the social level requires that the truth-seeker is obligated to take extreme care that one has truth on one's side, that injustice is in fact occurring, that injustice is causing significant damage to innocent individuals or to society and that the suffering imposed on oneself is a true and sincere act of love and not a vengeful show at heart.

The great effectiveness of the family situation assured the Mahatma of the effectiveness of truth-persistence. But he clearly laid down that the above precautions have to be taken just as they would be in the family situation. In an atmosphere marred by mutual distrust and lack of love, it would not be possible to transfer the success from the family level to the socio-political level. The key ingredient of genuine nonviolence is absent in such atmosphere.

Clearly, the effectiveness of truth-persistence is in direct proportion to the sincerity and love in the heart of the seeker. A seeker viewing the self-suffering merely as a tool to coerce the opponent's will would not succeed in changing the heart of the unjust opponent.

For the seeker, seeking the truth is its own end and reward. Indeed, one lives in truth while seeking it to the point of acute self-suffering. Truth-realization involved in this living is not less valuable than succeeding in bringing the truth about. When this point is seen to the core, one cannot be far from seeing the point of the Mahatma's philosophy as a whole.

CHAPTER FIVE

GANDHIJI'S THOUGHT AS A WHOLE

Let us now bring the Mahatma's thought together as a whole. We will articulate the central concepts of God, truth and nonviolence in the words of Kishorlal Mashruwala's *Quintessence of Gandhi's Thought.* This will be followed by an outline of all key concepts arranged and enunciated in a systematic manner to facilitate clear comprehension. Supporting reasons also will be shown in brief to bring out the cogency of the entire thought as a single coherent unit. Obviously, this will involve some restatement of points made hitherto, albeit in a brief form.

As explained earlier, Mashruwala's book in Gujarati is not available in English, though it is regarded by Gandhians as the Bible of Gandhism. It summarizes Gandhiji's thought covering all its topics and sub-topics. Mashruwala's work is aphoristic, systematic and ordered in a clear logical manner. Needless to say, all the changes recommended by Gandhiji have been incorporated in the work. Gandhiji himself approved the work as authentic and, in his forward to the book, credited Mashruwala's extraordinary grasp of his thought coupled with expressing it in a clear and accurate form.

The *Quintessence* is divided in fourteen parts titled as follows:

1. Spirituality

2. Spiritual Paths

3. Society

4. Truth-persistence

5. Self-rule

6. Commerce

7. Industry

8. Cow Care

9. Khaddar

10. Cleanliness and Health

11. Education

12, Literature and Art

13. Public Servant

14. Institutions.

The work obviously deals with an amazingly wide range of subjects. Each of the above fourteen parts is subdivided in several sections, with each section containing consecutively numbered statements. In the following, I will present my translation of the first three sections of the first part in full. Unfortunately, the translation of the full work has to await a future moment.

Gandhi-Vichar-Dohan

or

Quintessence of Gandhi's Thought

By Kishorlal G. Masruwala

Part One: Spirituality

Section 1

God

1. Realization of God is the only proper goal of life. All human efforts should but be the means to achieve it.

2. All actions contrary to this goal should be avoided, even when their outcome may look tempting.

3. On the other hand, every action which is a means to the goal must be performed, even if it involves hardship, risk or apparent damage.

4. The nature of God is beyond senses, speech and thought. But it can be experienced and recognized. There are two tips to recognizing it. One is trust and the other is the experiential knowledge that follows it. The greatest teachers of the world have vouched for their experience that this God is infinite, without beginning and always consistent. They have witnessed God as the essence, cause or ground of the universe. God is one with sentience and knowledge. God alone has eternal existence; all else is transitory. To understand this God with a little word, let us use the word "truth."

5. So, it is more proper to say that truth alone is God than that God alone is truth. This truth is not a material property but

is pure consciousness. It alone runs the world and is, therefore, God.

6. This mode of understanding is a way to feel the transcendental nature of truth that is God.

7. God can also be felt in a concrete way. Whatever action today appears to me to be so proper, just and right that I ought to do it, would not be ashamed of endorsing and performing it and would not be able to live in the world if I do not do it is truth for me. Just that is God's concrete form revealed to me.

8. Ceaselessly searching for this truth and diligently implementing as much of it as is found in whatever form is what is meant by insisting on truth; and this is the way to God-realization.

9. Truth is infinite and the universe is boundless. Hence, the search never comes to an end. It may, therefore, seem that complete realization of God is not possible. This is no excuse for dismay. Nor is it an excuse to start churning boundless waters from one's little point of view. One should rather experiment and search for truth in whatever big or small, important or seemingly trivial activities one has to do in life. One will find the truth this way with the maxim "as in microcosm, so in macrocosm."

10. No one who is an indifferent onlooker of untruth, injustice and wrong-doing going on around oneself can realize truth. Hence, truth-searcher will work intensely to eradicate such untruth, injustice and wrong-doing and will regard the search to be incomplete until success in the eradication through means such as truth is not secured. Thus, resisting of untruth, injustice and wrong-doing is part and parcel of insisting on truth.

11. All religions assert, history witnesses and experience affirms that it is fruitless to search for truth through means such as untruth and violence. It is also not possible to find truth

without purifying the mind through self-restraint, determination and devotion, which are, therefore, indispensable means to God-realization.

Section 2

Truth

1. That truth alone is God is the transcendental or higher understanding of truth. In the mundane everyday understanding, truth means insisting on truth through truthful thinking, truthful speech and truthful action.

2. "Satya," which means "truth," is derived from the root "sat," which means "to be." It always has and will have true being. "Asatya" or untruth means "non-being." It has no true being. It always perishes. Only the truth prevails. Truth alone is good and beneficial in the long run. "Satya" and "sat" also mean "good." Therefore, truthful thinking, speech and action and insisting on truth are at the same time good thinking, speech and action and insisting on the good.

3. Insisting on truth means ceaselessly searching for the true and eternal laws through which mechanical as well as purposeful aspects of the world system keep running, molding one's life in accordance with those laws and resisting untruth through means such as truth.

4. Truthful thinking is that thought which we find to be just and proper in all circumstances or for as far as it is possible to see in the circumstances, with the help of an impartial, confident and devoted mind emptied of passion and hatred.

5. Truthful speech is statement which, when duty calls, fully reports the facts just as they are known and does not make them appear different by adding or withholding anything.

6. Truthful action is the thoughtful implementation of truthful thought.

7. Say that the mundane, relative truth is the means and the transcendental, eternal truth is the end. Or, say that God-realization is perfect implementation of the mundane, relative truth through truthful thinking, truthful speech, truthful action and insisting on truth. The two are not different for a true devotee of truth.

Section 3

Nonviolence

1. Ordinarily, people identify truth just with its gross meaning of speaking the truth. But truth-speaking does not quite exhaust implementation of truth. Similarly, people identify *ahimsa* or nonviolence just with gross meaning of not taking life. But observance of nonviolence is not completed merely by not taking life.

2. Nonviolence is not simply a gross rule of behavior. It is rather an attitude of mind. Nonviolence is an attitude where there is not even a trace of hatred is left.

3. Such nonviolence is as pervasive as truth. It is impossible to realize truth without realizing such nonviolence. Hence, in a way, truth is the culmination of nonviolence. Perfected truth and total nonviolence are not distinct. Still, as an aid to understanding, it can be said that truth is the end and nonviolence is the means.

4. Truth and nonviolence are like two sides of the coin of eternal reality.

5. Many religions say that God is one with love. Nonviolence is not different from this love.

6. Nonviolence is the pure and pervasive form of love. Love that smacks of passion or infatuation is not nonviolence. Passion and infatuation harbor the seed of hatred. Love is often accompanied by passion and infatuation. That is why careful thinkers have avoided the word "love" to emphasize nonviolence as the highest duty.

7. The duty of nonviolence is not exhausted in not hurting another's body or mind which, though, can be generally regarded as a visible characteristic of the observance of nonviolence. It is possible that the duty of nonviolence is correctly discharged in cases where an apparent harm occurs to another's body or mind. On the contrary, it is possible that violence has been committed even if no visible ground can be found to sustain a charge of harm or suffering. Nonviolence exists not merely in its visible effects; it primarily resides in a state of consciousness which is devoid of passion or hatred.

8. Yet, visible characteristic is not to be neglected. For, even if it is a gross tool, it is generally useful to gauge the degree to which the attitude of nonviolence has developed in one's own or another's heart. Speech and action designed not to cause grievance to living beings are, in common life, a direct measure of the degree of nonviolence cultivated by a person. Incidents occur where nonviolence causes some suffering. For instance, fasting with a pure motive and for self-purification can exert a sort of pressure on someone who loves us; but one can clearly see nonviolence in this case. Total nonviolence is not possible where there is even a small trace of selfishness.

9. But this is not enough to conclude that complete nonviolence has been achieved. The true devotee of nonviolence is not content with avoiding speech and action that would cause grievance in others or even with removing all trace of hatred from one's mind. Rather, he or she will keep empathizing with the current suffering in the world, searching for the means to eliminate it and working to implement those meas. Moreover, he or she will be pleased to suffer for another's happiness. So,

nonviolence is neither a passive withdrawal nor an absence of action. On the contrary, it is a powerful activity or operation,

10. There is intense efficient energy in nonviolence. This unfailing energy is not fully researched yet. "Hatred and vengeance calm down in face of true nonviolence" is not a bookish precept but a sage's experiential wisdom. Knowingly or unknowingly, all beings spontaneously suffer for others. It is this suffering that really runs the world. Nonviolent energy is not fully exploited. The way to utilize it for all aims and ends is not consciously explored.

11. On the other hand, humans have for long exerted to explore and exploit the ways of violence. They have even succeeded in making violence into a pseudo-science. Instead, if we make comparable effort to cultivate and consolidate the energy of nonviolence, we will end up proving that nonviolence is an invaluable and unfailing instrument to eliminate human suffering, benefitting all the conflicting parties.

12. We need to research nonviolent energy and find means of applying its laws in practice, with the same faith and industry with which the scientist researches the energies of nature and tries to find practical uses of physical laws.

The above narration by Kishorlal-bhai speaks for itself, even as I struggled to accurately represent the original Gujarati which is very rich in suggestions. Its clarity, simplicity and depth are extraordinary. Kishorlal-bhai has indeed accomplished a mammoth task of distilling and articulating the meaning of the central operative concepts of truth and nonviolence of the Mahatma. Gandhiji's concept of God is shown to be the foundation of Gandhian spirituality which elevates an incredibly demanding ethic to the level of a religion.

Having seen an articulation of the Mahatma's core or primary concepts of truth and nonviolence in words approved by the Mahatma himself, let us turn to a brief survey of the auxiliary or the other key concepts in Gandhiji's thought. We will approach this task in two somewhat overlapping segments.

The first segment will attempt to see the auxiliary concepts as emanating from Gandhiji's dual concept of truth. It develops into a delineation of the conceptual surroundings and underpinnings of the life of Gandhian truth-seeking. Let us call this segment "Gandhian Truth in Its Conceptual Context."

The second segment is called "Action and Intuition: Mahatma Gandhi's Road to Truth." It will attempt to show a road-map, placing the personal, social and political concept clusters of the Mahatma's thinking into a pattern of intuition-based action on the part of the Gandhian truth-seeker. The personal or individual aspect covers the adherence to and cultivation of the resolves or vows. Social aspect lists items in the Gandhian constructive program. The political aspect refers to the civil disobedience action involved in Gandhian *satyagraha* or truth-persistence.

Gandhian Truth in Its Conceptual Context

Gandhiji's starting point is, of course, his highly non-understood and also quite misunderstood concept of truth. It is important to see that truth for him is intuited as having more intrinsic worth than anything else in the world. It is the highest value and human life is best dedicated to its pursuit. Nothing at all has more value in life. Everything we do in life should be as means to achieving the end of realizing this truth which is the same as God. For the Mahatma, truth so conceived is God, not the other way around.

Truth has two aspects. One is the essential or absolute aspect. The other is the existential or relative aspect. If the first is like the Sun, the second is like our little puddles where the Sun is reflected. If the first is like a parent, the second is like children. The first one, essential truth shows that essence comes before existence, as a whole, as space logically comes before matter which cannot exist without space. But as far as the human individual is concerned, existence comes before essence, as one's body usually comes before one's name.

Other way speaking, the essential truth is the infinite source of human sustenance and the ultimate ground of all human action, but it also is beyond language, concepts and reason. On the other hand, existential truth is the finite ground of particular action, being the concrete revelation of the essential to the humans.

As far as the essential aspect of truth is concerned, we should note its three constituents: being, awareness and joy. One may say it is these three in their infinite and pure forms. Because it is all-inclusive and pervasive, it cannot be boxed into one or even few categories or classes. So it is that it cannot be grasped by our little finite minds. Yet, it is the final goal for us all to realize. Essential truth is not just to be conceptualized, it is the highest end to be actually realized.

The essential truth equally informs and sustains all living beings for whom it is the foundation of their existence. Since it is equally the source of all, we can and should never use violence toward anyone. Just as we should not compromise truth in any way, we should not be violent toward anyone for any reason. But how do we get closer to this infinite essential truth whose scope is so overwhelming for us finite beings? The existential aspect of truth is there to give us a helping hand on this.

We saw that the essential reveals itself to us as existential. So, if we go by the existential truth, it will get us closer to the essential truth. Easy to say, but hard to do. Yet, the reward is worth all the effort. When the existential truth reveals the essential to us as ethically compelling action, we face three obstacles in seeing the truth.

For one, we are insensitive to taking of ethical action. We may tell ourselves that it is none of our business to lessen someone's suffering. We are desensitized by callousness or selfishness or plain simple laziness. Even a small action looks too big and daunting if it has to be done for others, especially strangers.

Second obstacle is impaired vision. We wear thick dark glasses of our vested interests that blur our vision. If we own shares of a corporation or are employed by one, we won't easily see that it is polluting the air or water or that it exploits a group or discriminates against minority.

Third obstacle is lack of strong will. We may see an untruth or injustice by getting sufficiently sensitive and clearing our truth vision. But we may not have the strength of the will to get off our seat and plunge into effective action. In support of our weak will, we may invent numerous excuses to reinforce our inaction. What about my children's future? Am I my brother's keeper? If I jeopardize my job by blowing the whistle on my boss, who will take care of my family, not to speak of myself?

How do we overcome these three obstacles? More obstacles may be lurking, too. How do we deal with them effectively? Mahatma Gandhi offers three avenues to wok on. At the personal level, we can and should practice certain observances. At the social level, we are invited to design and participate action lines in accordance with the constructive program of Gandhiji. At the political level, if and when there is a calling to that effect, we can participate in, or even plan and lead, a truth-persistence program or civil disobedience movement.

The next segment, called Mahatma Gandhi's Road to Truth, will get us more details on these three avenues to overcome obstacles in recognizing and overcoming obstacles to actional truth. As we prepare and get ready for action, we are going to begin our life as truth-seekers in Gandhian, or for that matter, any other ethical-spiritual way. What is life like in broad terms and features, for a Gandhian truth-seeker?

At the individual level, the truth-seeker is motivated toward an approximation of truth as God, not God as truth. While truth as God distinguishes a spirituality or spiritual path, God as truth marks a religion or a credal faith. Gandhiji's truth-seeking journey is a path that blends spirituality and ethics. If you want to add a religious flavor to it and it does not bring up any obstacles of its own to truth-seeking, Gandhiji won't mind it. But a narrow and exclusivist alley of a cult or sect may be a real obstacle to truth-seeking in the Gandhian sense of the term.

At the community level, the Mahatma advocates the ideal of *sarvodaya*, or the uplift of all, where no one in the community is left behind. Gandhiji got this idea from John Ruskin's book called *Unto This Last*. The principle as formulated by Gandhiji is that no one can be truly happy in a community where anyone else is unhappy. Hence, one's true happiness consists in having everyone in the community without exception getting uplifted.

One may say that this sounds good, but one may also have three major concerns. Call them specificity, conflict and identification. Let us see what they are and how a Gandhian truth-seeker would respond to them.

First, the concern or question of specificity. Specifically, it is that essential revealing itself in existential and guiding our life of truth-seeking in general is too abstract, ocean-wide and open-ended. It may include everything and hence, specifically, nothing. Why not specify particular course of action to perform for all times to come? Then we would know what to do at any given time.

This may be called the buy-and-hold strategy. You may have a small list of rules and abide by them forever. For one thing, such a plan is likely to be rigid and unrealistic. Life and world are not static. Change is the name of the game. Things move and change. We move and change too. Is there a short cut to keep up with the dynamism of life and reality? Flexibility, compromise and adjustment are called for so often in a single life time that even a large list of specific rules and ideas for guidance may be unable to keep up.

May I give an example from personal experience? In my youth I took one of the toughest examinations in the nation and passed it, to become a highly placed officer in the government. My job, with the help of my colleagues, was to enforce and administer direct taxes. The business community in the country, especially relating to the underground economy which wanted to evade taxes by concealing income through creative accounting, devised ever-new ways to show losses rather than income. Every year the government would pass legislation plugging the loopholes and regulating the new ways to conceal income. But the outside community would create newer and newer ways in their accounting to hide revenue or profit. One year it may be hundis, another year havala entries and so on. We were trained in investigative accounting to catch the miscreants, but they were clever enough to stay ahead of the game. The point is that untruth is not unintelligent or static so that a few simple rules can fix it. Even a battalion of moving rules are not enough, at times.

If a few, like, say, ten commandments could fix untruth, truth may have been the reigning king for thousands of years and there would be no need to create an extensive literature like the Talmud to interpret and understand the truth. Hence, specific actions as a standing and stand-alone remedy is unworkable. The ways of untruth are cleverly evasive. The truth-seeker has to be ever vigilant to detect them and try to eradicate them as they take root.

The second question pertains to conflict. Two sorts of conflict are under review: intra-personal and inter-personal. Suppose a person is conflicted within oneself. One's intuition asked to do one thing at a time. A similar situation arises after a few years but the intuition now asks to do another thing. Which one is right? Gandhiji himself faced this question, with people pointing out that he said one thing previously and was saying a different thing later. Gandhiji's answer was that the later had to be preferred to the former. His reason was that there was the presumption of growth in truth-perception. If one is a good truth-seeker, one grows with time in truth-vision and so the later vision is likely to be more accurate in seeing the truth.

Inter-personal conflict is a harder cookie to crack. What should be done if two or more persons or groups have conflicting intuitive visions of existential truth with regard to the same situation? If no negotiation, adjustment or compromise can be worked out and conflicts stare in the face, one can suggest some alleviating features. One is to respect the differences and do the best that can be done. Another is to take solace in the fact that the same essential truth inhabits all the existential truth observers so, again, all should be treated as having equally respectable truth under the unusual condition.

A third factor is that, after all, if all conflicting persons or groups stay nonviolent, it may be best to see whose heart gets transformed in what way and try to find some clue to resolve the differences. If the differences stay unresolved, one may do the best under the circumstances.

The fourth alleviating feature is to point out that, if all parties pursue only nonviolent actions, the violence resulting from the conflict would be no more than conceptual. The problem with human conflicts is with violence, mainly speaking. Lot of damage and evil result proceed directly from violence. When conflicts go without resolution but no violence occurs, damage is limited and the resultant learning is likely to be positive. So, overall, there is a distinct comparative advantage in nonviolent conflicts. Yes, the key and challenge is to stay nonviolent, with the understanding that violence is a mark of untruth which can never lead to truth.

The third question was about identification of the ethical. How is one to identify an action as ethical, let alone ethically compelling? Gandhian thinking has three responses: Negative criteria, positive criteria and constructive aspects.

Negative criteria would weed out options which are unacceptable for the truth-seeker. The foremost among them is violence. Any option involving violence is out right away. Another negative criterion is to see if an option serves the interests of the aggrieved in the situation. Options not serving the needs of the adversely impacted parties are filtered out by this criterion. Third test is coziness. Between an option that keeps one cozy and another that imposes some suffering, the latter is preferred by a Gandhian on the ground that voluntary suffering has a strengthening effect on the truth-seeker's character and personality. Makes one more tenacious.

Lack of self-shame is yet another negative criterion. Righteous self-shame is a positive aspect that makes for self-improvement. A shameless person is less likely to improve and make progress, if at all. Shame, properly used and understood, and when it is not just guilt, is a means by which a truth-seeker can make progress in the journey toward truth.

Fifth is the demanding situation criterion. If an option relates to a created situation rather than following from a demanding situation it should be filtered out. The truth-seeker should not participate in a situation where one becomes a hero in a situation created for the heroic display. Behaving fearlessly in a demanding situation is the opposite, helping the seeker to go further in the truth journey.

Coming to the positive criteria. Obviously needed action is one good clear positive criterion. An example is removal of prejudice. Another positive criterion is growing truth-perception. A sincere truth-seeker will make greater strides toward truth by progressively taking on more and more demanding situations and thereby improving one's truth-vision through increasingly concrete experience and experimentation.

Assiduous practice of observances helps one rise above truth-distorting self-interests. Particularly, as one faces difficulties that show up in the practice and overcomes them with tenacity. Further positive criteria include a disciplined life of interest-transcending as against a life of mere intellectual exercise. This helps gain real objectivity, distinct from just perceptual or even conceptual objectivity.

Gandhiji has an unfailing Talisman criterion too: Do that which serves most the needs of the most oppressed that you can find. Can be challenging indeed! But it also can be very rewarding in terms of moving closer to truth.

Among constructive aspects on the question of identifying the ethical are three points. One is that practicality is more promising than hypothetical posturing. Another is to exercise free individual choice in humble service of humanity. The spirit of service really helps pave the way toward truth. Third constructive aspect results from keeping in mind the actual advancement of the oppressed.

Action and Intuition: Mahatma Gandhi's Road to Truth

This segment lists details of the personal, social and political aspects of truth-seeking in the Gandhian spiritual journey. The prime mover toward essential truth, as we have seen, is the existential truth through the unending series of ethically compelling actions. Hence, action is the key. While doing ethically compelling actions is the highway toward truth, being in shape to perform them when it is demanded of oneself is of practical importance. Preparing the ground for it through keen observation of the community is also important.

In this light, action needed to be done, as an aggregate, can be divided in three areas: Bodily action, observative action and performative action. Bodily action in the context of truth-seeking roughly pertains to maintenance of bodily functions and cleanliness. Observative action can be addressed to the self or the public. Observing oneself and accounting to oneself on a regular basis are necessary. Details can be worked out as appropriate and needed, by oneself or in the company of associates.

Observing the community is a highly valuable aspect of public observative action. This should be done with a keen eye to perceive and detect instances of injustice or untruth happening in the society. Keeping abreast of what is going on in the community, diligently and with vigilance, aids in seeing significant patterns of wrong-doing.

Gandhiji put inordinate emphasis on accounting to the public. He and his associates kept careful and scrupulous accounts of every penny spent from all the money donated by the public. The Mahatma openly and publicly reprimanded all lapses, even seeming lapses or perceptions of impropriety. Examples abound when he would take a matter of few pennies extremely seriously and would not be restrained from vituperating Kasturba in public if he found any irresponsible spending of public's money entrusted to the commune. Transparency was a policy dictate for him for the *ashram* life.

Performative action obviously holds the greatest significance in the context of truth-seeking in the Gandhian style. It can be divided in three types for the sake of clear understanding: purificatory or micro, constructive or standard and dramatic or macro.

Purificatory action cleans the mind and prepares an individual for the spiritual journey of truth-seeking. It consists of observances or vows. At both individual and group level one of its major ingredients was prayer. One should pray individually and privately. One also should participate in mass prayers where members of the commune get together to pray every morning and evening. Prayer, according to Gandhiji, brings one close to truth and helps develop one's intuition through inspiration and building of spiritual resource.

At the individual level, there are several vows. The famous Gandhian count is eleven resolves to be kept by all in a disciplined way and stringently. No violations are permitted. All transgressions have to be accounted for publicly at the prayer meetings and have to be atoned for as the community decides.

These are the eleven vows for all individuals:

1. Truth

2. Nonviolence

3. Non-stealing

4. Non-hoarding

5. Continence

6. Bread labor

7. Nondiscrimination

8. Fearlessness

9. Community products

10. Control of appetite

11. Equal respect for all religions.

Performative action's constructive aspect consists of standard social action for the truth-seeker. It used to be defined as the fourteen-point constructive program. Here is an extended version listing eighteen areas:

1. Communal unity

2. Removal of untouchability

3. Handspun clothing

4. Other rural industries

5. Village sanitation

6. New or basic education

7. Adult education

8. Uplift of women

9. Education in health and hygiene

10. Provincial languages

11. National language

12. Economic equality

13. Uplift of farmers

14. Uplift of laborers

15. Uplift of tribals

16. Treatment of lepers

17. Welfare of students

18. Improvement of cattle.

The idea of constructive program was conceived as the social activity area for the Gandhian truth-seeker. Of course, its contents and coverage would be different for different communities, cultures, societies and countries. They could also change over time. This eighteen-point structure is for illustrative purposes only. Items would be added or deleted on the basis of actual social need at the time of implementation. The idea should be dynamic and flexible, based on the preparedness of the community of truth-seekers.

Obviously, not every truth-seeker is expected to do work in all the items. Personal preference and individual choice may be used to fill the work allotment. Alternatively, if there is imbalance, rotation of workers may be used to achieve functionality.

The list may be used by an unaffiliated truth-seeker in the Gandhian style to select areas where one may want to contribute. Alternatively, one may use it to find areas of need where one may find contributors to recruit. There are many creative areas and avenues for doing positive and constructive work by conscientious social workers, not just Gandhian truth-seekers.

The dramatic aspect of performative action is the participation in a civil disobedience movement or *satyagraha* plan of action. Gandhiji called this *satyagraha* or insistence on truth. It has been called truth force, but that does not seem to catch the meaning and intent of the Mahatma's conception. "Truth-persistence" perhaps gets the most of the intent behind the term *satyagraha.*

The need for a *satyagraha* plan of political action arises from situation. The idea should not be applied to created situations. In the Mahatma's view it may arise from purificatory action, constructive action or external contingencies. Strong effort should be made to keep it within well-defined boundaries of nonviolence. Gandhiji has written extensively about the needed behavior of both participants and leaders of a *satyagraha* program and strategy.

Ethically compelling action, being an individual's particular revelation of essential truth in the form of an existential truth for oneself, is an intuition from the viewpoint of the individual. In other words, the individual intuits the actional revelation. Or, the action appears to the individual as the moment's or situation's existential truth.

Is this different from the concept of conscience or calling spoken of in many a religious and spiritual tradition? It is at least akin to them or has all the appearances of conscience or calling. It's like an inner voice with a compelling impact. It shames the individual, in a way, making one to feel guilty if the action urged is not performed. Yes, the conscience does not always appear in the form of action, as it must to a Gandhian. True, calling does appear as a plan of action. But mostly it is about choosing a vocation such as ministry.

Conscience has been understood or interpreted as the voice of God or some sort of a divine message. It has even been called a voice of reason. It is hard to say that the Mahatma would register a serious objection to interpretations that just conceptually seem to deviate from his own mode of understanding it as concrete existential appearance of the essential or transcendental truth. For him, its consistency and performance are truly important, what you call it or how you conceptualize it holds at best a secondary significance.

Similar will be the situation where the existential call for action is taken to be a communication from the inner self. Such an understanding may be friendlier to someone with an agnostic or even atheistic background. Gandhiji was never attracted to atheism of any sort. Still, he was able to work closely with many a humanitarian and conscientious persons with nontheistic tendencies. The conceptual form that an individual's spiritual journey takes was of less significance to him than the substance and patterns of actions.

Revelatory interpretation is a form of intuition, being a direct internal perception in the mind. To call the revelation an appearance of essential truth or God is Gandhiji's own conceptual formulation, if you will, that is strikingly original because of its actional and ethical attire. There is no way to go around or ignore the innovative character of the existential side of Gandhiji's dual concept of truth.

So also is the Mahatma's notion of the growth of intuition. Applying the idea of growth to the actional intuition ensures flexibility and dynamism to the Gandhian spiritual process in the mind, heart and soul of the truth-seeker. Because Gandhiji conceives the process as unending, a solid sense of progression and continuous improvement adds a substantially positive dimension to the spiritual journey, increasing faith and confidence with time as the seeker takes on more and more difficult situations and overcomes the obstacles in the path. Let us end this journey into Gandhiji's thought on this constructive note!

ABOUT THE AUTHOR

Ramesh N. Patel is well-equipped to write about a universal interfaith spirituality which is greatly needed at this point in time when the world is strife-torn, embattled and polarized for longer than we can bear. His path to this point in his life has been a long and checkered one. Here are some details.

Ramesh was Professor of Philosophy and Religion at Antioch College, Yellow Springs, Ohio for twenty-five years. He retired in 2002. At school, five Sanskrit teachers showered grace on him to instill Panini's *vyakarana*, the greatest grammar in the world, in his mind. Armed with it, he went ahead to earn B.A. and M.A. in Sanskrit at the University of Bombay, in St. Xavier's College. He received several honors, distinctions, prizes and scholarships for his performance in Sanskrit. He was appointed a Fellow in Sanskrit at St. Xavier's. His specialization at M.A. was "Veda and Comparative Philology." He took his LL.B. from Government Law College at the University of Bombay. Abandoning his doctoral work on "Anomalous Grammatical Forms in Rigveda," he joined Indian administrative service as Class One Income Tax Officer for six years, during which period he found time to do doctoral work on "The Problem of Universals in Modern Analytic Philosophy" and on "Rational Philosophy in Sanskrit."

He came to the U.S.A. where he earned M.A. and Ph.D. in Western philosophy at the University of New Mexico. His master's thesis was called "A Critique of Logical Atomism." His doctoral dissertation was titled "A Constructive Critique of the Foundations of Philosophy." He taught philosophy at Lake Forest College for six years before arriving at Antioch College in 1976.

Ramesh taught more than seventy different courses in Eastern, Western and comparative philosophy and religion, thus becoming a generalist rather than a specialist. Antioch's emphasis on teaching allowed him to focus on teaching a wide variety of courses, but he found time to write, present and publish papers in philosophy and religious studies. He taught courses in all the historical periods of Western philosophy including contemporary analytic philosophy, phenomenology and existentialism. He taught numerous courses connecting philosophy with other academic disciplines, for example, philosophy of art, of history, of language, law, mind, religion, physical sciences, social sciences and so on. He taught courses in world religions and comparative religious studies. Besides philosophy and religion, he also taught courses in meditation, music, financial management, business ethics and personal finance. His most notable experience at Antioch was his course called Gandhi: Truth and Nonviolence, which he taught for eighteen years.

Ramesh is uncomfortable with just lecturing. He feels as if he is talking to himself when he lectures and audience just listens. He provokes his audience with constantly playing Devil's advocate to gaud them into thinking for themselves. He wants them to ask whatever questions that arise in their minds. He prefers to flow freely but discursively with discussions. Not just his students, he claims he has himself benefited a great deal in terms of sharpened thinking on a variety of topics as they get discussed intensively in the classes through this Socratic method of discursive teaching.

Ramesh owned a small business in nearby Fairborn, Ohio for thirty-three years. His wife Kanta ran the business, while Ramesh pursued his academic interests. Ramesh also has taught at Union Theological Seminary and Wittenberg University. After retiring from Antioch, Ramesh has continued to teach under the auspices of the Hindu Temple of Dayton, voluntary adult courses in Bhagavad-Gita, Hinduism, Upanishads, Vedic philosophy and spirituality studies.

Ramesh has written and presented several articles in philosophy and religion. His book *Philosophy of the Gita* was published in 1990. He published his book *Hinduism for Today* in 2012. Besides his wide-ranging interests in philosophy and religious studies, Ramesh has his own philosophy which he calls "logical meta-philosophy." Over years he has enriched this philosophy with influences from Mahatma Gandhi and Pandit Madhusudan Ojha. He invites anyone and everyone to engage him in philosophy, particularly philosophy of spirituality and enduring issues in logical meta-philosophy. He can be contacted at rameshphilosophy@gmail.com.

Ramesh very recently published his third book, called *One Being: Spiritual Path of Adi Shankara.* It deals with the spirituality and its underlying philosophy of Adi Shankara who is regarded as the foremost spiritual leader and philosopher in India's long history. Its message of unity in diversity is not only a burning need of the times: it is presented with a strong rationale to back it up.

Ramesh published his fourth book more recently. It's called *Self and World: Major Aspects of Indian Philosophy.* Among philosophies introduced and described in the book are Yoga, Vedanta, four Buddhist systems and Jainism. Yoga is rightly celebrated for its spiritual and psychological healing effects. Vedanta is widely recognized for its universal spiritual reach and for its friendly demeanor toward all other world faiths. Buddha's message of universal compassion and Jainism's legendary insistence on non-violence are appreciated globally.

One feature of this book that stands out is its salient outline of Vedic philosophy as unearthed by Pandit Madhusudan Ojha in the twentieth century. This is an unknown and unsung but comprehensive and coherent philosophy that is the first chapter in the history of systematic philosophy in the world. It influenced all other thought that occurred in India, including Yoga, Vedanta, Buddhism and Jainism. A detailed outline of this vast philosophy, so far unknown to scholars, is accorded an entire chapter in the book. A glossary of Sanskrit terms with explanations at the end of the book should be very useful for those needing help getting into the deeper meanings of several spiritual philosophies included in the book with great healing potential and relevance for our troubled times.

Ramesh published his fifth book even more recently. It is called "Spiritual Stories: Inspiring Messages of Wisdom." It is his first attempt in the genre of fiction. Ramesh has been a story teller since his childhood. In this book he has collected twenty-seven stories from his large repertoire. Each story contains an inspiring message of wisdom, may it relate to commonsense, morality or spirituality. The stories all pertain to spiritual aspects in one form or another. They span a variety of subjects including self-transformation, God, guru, karma, virtues and human follies. Extended life-stories of two remarkable women, Draupadi and Meera, are also included. The book can be read with joyful learning by people of all ages.

Ramesh published his sixth book even more recently. It is called *Hindu Philosophy of Life: Meaning of Life in Hinduism*. It is a solid introduction to Hinduism, the oldest living major religion of the world. The book brings out the stand-out features of Hinduism which are quite a few. It develops a clear and coherent four-point definition of Hinduism that many scholars have been unable to devise. It also organizes a sixteen-point thematic exposition of foundations of Hinduism that neatly outlines the principal aspects of meaningful life for Hindus. The book also emphasizes how Hinduism retains spirituality in Hindu life more than other religions of the world.

Drawing upon his long experience of teaching comparative world religions, Ramesh wants to write about universal time-tested features of different spiritualities of the world. He wants to integrate these commonalities in a structure that would help today's conflicting religions and warring groups of people to close their gaps and bring them together. Such healing common humanity of deep spiritual experience, sometimes buried deep in religious scriptures, needs to be brought out for the world to heal itself from its polarizing traumas. In current times this is relevant and crucial.

Ramesh is an independent thinker. He believes in everyone developing their own thinking. That is why he often plays Devil's advocate, even though it may be inconvenient or even irritating to some. Independent thinking does not mean just any kind of thinking goes. It means also responsible thinking, which requires giving reasons to support the thinking. Ramesh can be iconoclastic, rebellious, breaking norms, going against conventional wisdom, not going by political correctness. He is critical of dogmatism everywhere, in academia, political class, even in professional philosophy where much dogmatism goes on in the name of reason itself.

Ramesh likes all to be able to express themselves giving their reasons to support their thinking and be part of the world of discourse. He won't accept any authority, for we should be guided by reason, experience and value in our search for truth and reality. Mere opinions do not count. wherever they come from. Reason to support the statements is what is important. Again, giving of reasons to support a statement gives you admittance into the world of discourse. Weighing with counter-reasons as the next stage leads to better evaluation of the statement. Ramesh likes to present his reasons for his statements. Participants in discourse then should consider and weigh them. Ramesh does not want his readers to just accept his statements; he would like them to ponder his statements. Well-considered rejection can be preferable than blind acceptance.

Ramesh welcomes any comments, thoughts or suggestions on what may be of interest to his readers and all others interested in spirituality and philosophy. He enjoys teaching which he has done continuously since 1968. He enjoys music, both light and classical, particularly Hindustani and Bollywood oldies. You can also engage him in structuring your investment portfolio for retirement or financial freedom. Or, engage him in what you are interested. He will probably find something in his repertoire to link with it! Years ago he composed a Sanskrit verse and it may be a good way to end this biographical sketch:

Jyotir-mayi bhavatu jivana-madhuri te.

May sweetness and light pervade your life!

www.ingramcontent.com/pod-product-compliance
Ingram Content Group UK Ltd.
Pitfield, Milton Keynes, MK11 3LW, UK
UKHW021651190726
13853UKWH00001B/185

9 798686 070899